Animal Farm

George Orwell

Guide written and developed by
John Mahoney and Stewart Martin

First published 1987
Reprinted 1992

Illustration: Peter McClure

The authors and publishers are grateful to the Estate of Sonia Brownell Orwell and A M
Heath & Company Limited for permission to quote from *Animal Farm* by George Orwell,
published by Secker and Warburg Ltd.

Stewart Martin is an Honours graduate of Lancaster University, where he read English
and Sociology. He has worked both in the UK and abroad as a writer, a teacher, and an
educational consultant. He is married with three children, and is currently deputy
headmaster at Ossett School in West Yorkshire.

John Mahoney has taught English for twenty years. He has been head of English
department in three schools and has wide experience of preparing students at all levels
for most examination boards. He has worked both in the UK and North America
producing educational books and computer software on English language and literature.

British Library Cataloguing in Publication Data
Mahoney, John
Animal Farm: George Orwell: guide. –
(Guides to literature)
I. Orwell, George. Animal Farm
I. Title II. Martin, Stewart
III. Orwell, George IV. Series
823'.912 PR6029.R8A7

ISBN 1 85758 130 X

Printed and bound in Great Britain by
Staples Printers St Albans Ltd

Contents

To the student

This study companion to your English literature text acts as a guide to the novel or play being studied. It suggests ways in which you can explore content and context, and focuses your attention on those matters which will lead to an understanding, appreciative and sensitive response to the work of literature being studied.

Whilst covering all those aspects dealt with in the traditional-style study aid, more importantly, it is a flexible companion to study, enabling you to organize the patterns of study and priorities which reflect your particular needs at any given moment.

Whilst in many places descriptive, it is never prescriptive, always encouraging a sensitive personal response to a work of literature, rather than the shallow repetition of others' opinions. Such objectives have always been those of the good teacher, and have always assisted the student to gain high grades in 16+ examinations in English literature. These same factors are also relevant to students who are doing coursework in English literature for the purposes of continual assessment.

The major part of this guide is the 'Commentary' where you will find a detailed commentary and analysis of all the important things you should know and study for your examination. There is also a section giving practical help on how to study a set text, write the type of essay that will gain high marks, prepare coursework and a guide to sitting examinations.

Used sensibly, this guide will be invaluable in your studies and help ensure your success in the course.

George Orwell

George Orwell's real name was Eric Blair. He was born in Bengal, India in 1903. His father was a minor official in the Indian Civil Service.

When he was eight, his mother brought him and his two sisters to England; Orwell was sent to be educated at a boarding school on the south coast, where he remained until he was twelve.

In 1917 he won a scholarship to Eton, where he stayed until 1921. Instead of going to university, he joined the Indian Imperial Police in Burma. He felt that the British rule in India was wrong and he did not enjoy the part he had to play in exercising power as a policeman. He resigned his post in 1927 and then spent some time living amongst the poor workers and tramps in Paris and London. His first book, which was about those experiences, was called *Down and Out in Paris and London* and published in 1933.

In 1936 he set out for Spain to report on the Spanish Civil War. He soon found himself fighting on the Republican side, and was seriously wounded. The manipulation of the Republican side by communist groups and the purges that took place greatly affected him, and he left Spain in 1937.

His experiences of colonial rule and exploitation in India and what he saw as the betrayal of a revolution in Spain are directly reflected in his satire on the Russian Revolution in his novel *Animal Farm*, which was published in 1945. It is, however, a satire that has relevance to all political systems but especially to those which give a totality of power to one man or a small group of men.

His concern with such authoritarian societies led to the writing of *Nineteen Eighty-Four*, published in 1949. This book was concerned with a future society where personal freedom was totally at the mercy of the 'State'. It is in *Nineteen Eighty-Four* that we find the origin of the phrase 'Big Brother is watching you'.

George Orwell died in 1950.

OLD MAJOR TELLS THE OTHER ANIMALS OF HIS DREAM.

ALL ANIMALS ARE EQUAL

BUT

SOME ANIMALS ARE MORE EQUAL THAN OTHERS

THE BATTLE OF THE COWSHED

THE WILD ANIMALS ARE CONFUSED BY THE SEVEN COMMANDMENTS

NAPOLEON AND MR. PILKINGTON BOTH PLAY THE ACE OF SPADES

NAPOLEON CONSPIRES WITH MR. WHYMPER WHILE MOSES TELLS LIES ABOUT THE SUGAR CANDY MOUNTAIN

The Seven Commandments

1. Whatever goes on two legs is an enemy.
2. Whatever goes upon four legs or has wings is a freind.
3. No animal shall wear clothez.
4. No animal shall sleep in a bed. WITH SHEETS
5. No animal shall drink alcohol. TO EXCESS
6. No animal shall kill any other animal. WITHOUT CAUSE
7. All animals are equal.

THE CAT ATTEMPTS TO EXPLAIN COMRADESHIP TO THE BIRDS.

Peter McClure 1986

Understanding Animal Farm

An exploration of the major topics and themes in the novel

A knowledge of those events and characters from the Russian Revolution on which George Orwell modelled much of *Animal Farm* provides a useful background. However, the student should be aware that he is first and foremost concerned with the study of a work of fiction. Any coursework or examination answers that ignore the story and concentrate only on the historical origins will not gain high marks.

The following notes outline such historical background as will help the student to understand what George Orwell was trying to say in his book, but they also relate to the literary aspects of the novel.

Summaries of themes

The Rebellion

Animalism Animalism is based on Old Major's teaching in the same way that communism is presumed to be based on the teachings of Karl Marx. However, communism can mean different things to different people and societies. Such countries as the USSR or China, Yugoslavia or Poland are as much influenced by the individuals running them and the national characteristics of each, as they are by the doctrine of communism.

It is a mistake to consider *Animal Farm* as limited to being just a satire on communism. Animalism would now be interchangeable with a whole range of 'isms': fascism, socialism, conservatism, flat-earthism or whatever; it is not necessarily the system that is corrupt or faulty, but the individuals in power. Old Major, with all his good intentions, took no note of a crucial fact: whilst *his* ideals were sound and moral, corrupt individuals found ways and opportunities to exploit those ideals to suit their own purposes. *Animal Farm* shows that process in operation.

What is tragic is that many politicians and leaders still continue to look for such solutions, or 'isms', to their country's problems and the people still continue to be as exploited as the animals.

Corruption Corruption means moral deterioration, which is exactly what happens to the ideals of the Rebellion and to the pigs.

Animal Farm plots Napoleon's decline into the seven deadly sins: pride, lust, envy, gluttony, anger, laziness, and desire for your neighbours' goods. You might like to try to identify the times and occasions that Napoleon indulges himself in each of the sins. Also note the circumstances and any 'reasons or excuses' he may give to justify what he does.

You should note the instances of corruption as they occur throughout the story and trace the way in which it gradually affects every animal, either as one of those who suffer because of it, or those who gain from it. Look, for example, at how clothing has a lot to do with identity and certain personality traits. There is a vanity and superficiality in Mollie and Napoleon's favourite sow in the clothes they choose to wear. Jones and Napoleon as owner/rulers of Manor Farm are linked by their shared wardrobe, Napoleon's vanity is well illustrated in the scene where he dresses in a 'black coat, ratcatcher breeches, and leather leggings'. Food and drink as basic currencies of living recur as images of corruption throughout the story. The way they are dealt with indicates much of what is happening. Alcoholic drink is a symbol of corruption and is a measure of the pigs' downhill slide into moral deterioration.

History rewritten

Throughout *Animal Farm* events are rewritten according to the prevailing political needs of the pigs. To an extent it is a comment on the way we have of looking back on the 'good old days' that did not really exist. The great Elizabethan Age of the 16th century in England was fine for the comparatively few involved in exploration, theatre, science and so on, but not so good for the mass of people – especially if they followed what was considered to be the 'wrong' religion, were supposedly involved in treason, or (most likely of all) were just poor.

In *Animal Farm*, though, the 'good old days' are not remembered with any degree of clarity, and the pigs rather turn the idea on its head by referring to the bad old days of life under Mr Jones. They are always trying to make them seem worse than they were so as to make their own cruel excesses more acceptable to the animals. As is mentioned under the section on 'Communication', the control of books, thought and historical perspective is an essential part of the stock-in-trade of authoritarian social systems, and they often literally have their history books rewritten to show events as they want them to be rather than as they actually were.

The Seven Commandments

The constitution of Animal Farm is contained in the Seven Commandments, but it is slowly corrupted, with the original meaning gradually being changed over the course of a few years. Eventually none of Old Major's revolutionary principles remain and the last Commandment, which, of course, is a creation of the corrupt pigs, is simply a licence for them to do as they please. This is especially ironic as originally it was assumed that it was man who was to be feared and that free from man's tyranny a new and just society could flourish!

The Seven Commandments are ideals, rather than actual, practical commands, that would have been accessible to the working animals, expecially given their reluctance or inability to master the processes of education. However, perhaps if they had been kept the Rebellion might have worked; what do you think?

As you read the novel you should be aware of the processes by which the high ideals of Old Major were first translated into a set of Seven Commandments, and then gradually changed, eroded or just ignored over the course of the events at Animal Farm. There is a nice parallel here, of course, with the Ten Commandments in which so many of Western social, ethical and religious beliefs find their origins. Just as in *Animal Farm*, the Commandments have been watered down, reinterpreted, or just ignored to suit the beliefs of individuals or institutions.

Utopia

Utopia literally means 'no place' and originated with Sir Thomas More in 1516, who wrote of an imaginary island where a perfect society flourished.

Old Major envisaged Manor Farm as a 'Utopia'; examine closely the original Commandments and his speech to catch the flavour of his vision. However, for Utopia to flourish, it needs more than a vision. Does it need perfect men, or just men who are not corrupt – or is this the same thing? It is a very difficult idea to grasp and does not admit of an easy solution. You would do well to consider the extent to which the failure of the Animal Farm Utopia finds its parallels in the society in which we live and see if that consideration helps you to understand about what makes an imperfect society.

In George Orwell's *Animal Farm*, the failure of his Utopia, like so many others, is more due to individuals being imperfect, rather than the chosen system being at fault. Ultimately, you always have to recognize the fact that any social system is only as good as the people who operate it.

Communication

Fable and allegory

The novel is subtitled 'A Fairy Story', a type of story you will be familiar with from your earliest years. However, Orwell is being rather tongue-in-cheek when he uses that description. *Animal Farm* is much more of a fable, though it has to be said that there can be a great deal of overlap between the two types of story.

A fable is a fictional story, often using animals for characters, that has a moral. It is a way of making a moral point in an entertaining and acceptable way. An allegory is the story of one subject in the disguise of another. *Animal Farm* has both elements, and we cannot doubt that the author was attempting to make some specific comments about the nature of society and the people who comprise it. In reading the book you should have a mind open to the implications of what the author is saying, because there are many quite biting comments which all of us could well do to take to heart. Look for example at the chapter where he describes the animals' attitudes to being educated. The novel, *Animal Farm*, is not well served if you view it simply as a satire on the Russian Revolution.

Language   George Orwell was very conscious of the interaction between thought and opinion and language. He said of *Animal Farm* that it was 'The only one of my books I really sweated over'. He was fully conscious that he tried 'to fuse political and artistic purpose into one whole'.

In that sense Orwell was engaged in something of a propaganda exercise, although that is being somewhat simplistic about it. However, given that propaganda is the making known of a particular idea, doctrine, policy, opinion or whatever, with the idea of converting people to it, then the pigs of *Animal Farm* excel as propagandists. What was it that allowed Boxer, Clover and the other animals to be taken in to such an extent that they elevated Napoleon almost to the position of a god? In attempting to answer a question such as this you should note the tools of propaganda: the emotions of fear and anger, patriotism, misinformation, and control of basic needs in the areas of food and education which can be used to 'persuade' individuals towards the propagandist's viewpoint.

All of Squealer's speeches are propaganda, as are Napoleon's. Less directly it could be argued that so are Moses the raven's. You ought to read and study what they say very carefully, and try to identify the methods of persuasion they use to gain the animals' support.

Careful note should be taken of Snowball's attempt to educate the animals. It is not all that long ago when the majority of people could not read and write. It is perhaps not insignificant, however, that in modern times control of the written word, and latterly any means of mass communication, is the first target of any budding dictator or power-hungry politician. In a society where the demands on citizens require more and more a greater fluency in literacy, those who fail to become educated in this area put themselves at the mercy of their fellows. The failure to use your brain, allowing others to think for you, being satisfied with the 'rubbish heap' as the main source of news (as was Muriel the goat), being indifferent to the possibilities of education, does a disservice not only to yourself but to the whole of society. Note how the animals react to Snowball's educational ideals and how they suffer for their failures in the long term.

Satire   The satire of *Animal Farm* is partly that animals are put into a human situation but with
and irony their own well-known, associated strengths and weaknesses. Note the characters they enact. What qualities do we associate with pig, sheep, hen, etc, and how well do they live up, or down, to their reputations?

Part of the aim of putting animals into a human situation is to gain sympathy for them and to make them more entertaining. George Orwell was perhaps able to write more critically and bitingly under the guise of an animal tale. Few politicians would own to being like a pig!

Much of the success of the satire is that animals stay animals and their suffering is that of farm animals. They stay and act much as we would expect their species to act, so the shock of pig turning into man is very much greater when it happens in the last paragraphs of the story.

As with all satires, *Animal Farm* can be read at several interrelating levels of meaning and interpretation. It can be seen as a fable; an account of the Russian Revolution and its aftermath; the abuse of power (by whoever has the power); an exploration of social change and political expediency; or the rise to power of a dictator (as shown by Napoleon).

The ultimate irony is the last scene, when pig becomes man, in that Old Major at the beginning assumes that man is the only enemy of animals. He emphasizes that animals must never imitate man, especially his vices. Gradually in their life-style and their indifference to the animals, the pigs exploit the animals more than Jones ever did.

Songs and poems   The unifying and rallying effect of 'Beasts of England' is a strong influence on the working animals – too strong for Napoleon to tolerate. The powerful effect of patriotic or revolutionary songs is well illustrated here. Equally the point is made that such an effect is based upon free creativity and cannot be made to order, as in Minimus's feeble attempts at the same thing, the results of which sound ludicrous. It is not that 'Beasts of England' is high art, but that it is sincere and expresses a genuine ideal with which the animals can identify.

Conflicts

Fights and battles   These follow the history of Russia at key points during and after the 1917 Revolution. The first uprising by the Russian people against the Czar and the army took everyone by surprise, just as the animals' revolution happened on the spur of the moment, taking them and Mr Jones by surprise.

The Battle of the Cowshed echoes the attempts by 'White Russians', with some support from other European countries, to retake control from the Bolsheviks. Trotsky proved his military skill at this time which probably incurred the jealousy and hatred of Stalin. The parallel can easily be seen in the final relationship between Snowball and Napoleon.

The Battle of the Windmill was on a scale not previously experienced by the farm animals. It has its basis in the invasion of Russia by Germany in 1941, made without declaration of war upon a nominal ally. The Russian 'scorched earth policy' combined with heroic stands at Stalingrad and Leningrad, together with a terrible Russian winter, was finally victorious. The cost of twenty million Russian lives and the searing memory of all-out war on Russian soil helps us to understand the acceptance by the Russians (or farm animals) of such a harsh leadership.

The events of the Russian Revolution are fascinating reading, but as stated elsewhere in this section, you are studying a work of literature. You are therefore advised to become better acquainted with *Animal Farm* than with the details of the Russian Revolution for the purposes of assessment on an English literature course.

The knoll

The knoll is a potent image for the strong feeling that the Russian people have for their land. This is something more fundamental than patriotism and is akin to the emotion felt by children for parents and grandparents in a closely united family. Notice the close ties the animals have for the knoll. They race to it in their excitement at a successful expulsion of Mr Jones to view the land they now control. It is the place to which they return after the great purge, in sadness and fear. Notice how Clover, the great mother-figure in *Animal Farm*, is closely associated with the knoll.

Meetings

The meetings throughout the story register the early successes of the Rebellion and the emergence of their animal society. They also record Napoleon's crucial expulsion of Snowball and the long, downward movement of the animals' loss of power and their gradual enslavement. Who is at each meeting, where they are seated in relation to each other, the purpose and the consequences of each meeting are of major importance and you should be familiar with them.

The windmill

The windmill theme represents the planned industrialization of Russia after the Revolution in 1917. This includes the development of new industries and the collectivization of farms when they were gathered into vast cooperatives. This was organized under a series of Five-Year Plans. Peasants who opposed collectivization were treated similarly to the hens who opposed Napoleon's proposed plan to use their eggs for trade.

The difference between Snowball and Napoleon's aims for the use of the windmill's power refers to the changes of policies between the first and the last of the Five-Year Plans in Russia, as more realistic targets were set in the light of experiences gained and knowledge acquired, and with the shift of emphasis away from the ordinary people's needs to those of the international political struggles of major powers as we know it today. The relevance to *Animal Farm* can be seen quite clearly.

The first destruction of the windmill by the storm was a representation of the collapse of the Five-Year Plan's aims and objectives due to bad luck, lack of up-to-date knowledge and deficient expertise.

The blowing up of the windmill by Frederick refers to Germany's invasion of Russia in 1941 in breech of the pact made between the two countries. Napoleon's attempts to play off Frederick against Pilkington approximate to Stalin's negotiations with Germany and the Western Allies.

After the destruction of the windmill, Frederick and his men are astonished by the force of the animals' attack. This certainly equates with the Russian people's extraordinary courage and endurance in the Second World War when the Germans invaded, and each Russian city was held by the army and civilians at enormous cost. Even Napoleon/Stalin was involved in the fighting. What did unite leaders and people was an intense patriotism: hence the success of propaganda which exploits the notion of an external enemy. Napoleon capitalized on the animals' 'patriotism' with his constant but ludicrous witch-hunt for the absent Snowball.

Analysis chart

	Dates	First year: Early March		3 nights later	Passage of 3 months	23 June–Midsummer's Eve	24 June				Late summer	12 October	Winter	Second year: January		End of spring	3rd Sunday after Snowball expelled	Spring and summer	Late summer	
	Important events	Old Major's meeting – the dream	First singing of 'Beasts of England'	Old Major dies	The evolution of Animalism	The Rebellion	The Seven Commandments	Getting in the harvest	Snowball's classes	Napoleon 'educates' the puppies	Jones looks for help	Battle of the Cowshed	Mollie runs away	The pigs take over decision-making	Snowball's plans for the windmill	Snowball expelled from Animal Farm	Napoleon announces windmill to be built	Work starts on the windmill	Napoleon announces trade with other farms	First visit of Whymper. Pigs move into farmhouse
	Chapter	1		2				3			4		5					6		
Themes	The Rebellion	●		●				●			●		●					●		
	Meetings	●		●				●			●		●					●		
	Conflicts			●							●									
	Communications	●		●				●			●		●					●		
	The knoll			●									●							
	The windmill												●					●		
Characters	Old Major	●		●									●							
	Snowball			●				●			●		●							
	Napoleon	●		●				●			●		●					●		
	Squealer			●				●			●		●					●		
	Boxer	●		●				●			●		●					●		
	Clover	●		●				●					●					●		
	Benjamin	●						●			●							●		
	Moses	●		●																
	Muriel																			
	Mollie	●		●				●			●		●							
	The sheep	●						●					●							
	Mr Jones	●		●							●		●							
	Pilkington and Frederick										●							●		
	Mr Whymper																	●		
	Page in commentary on which chapter first appears	21		25				31			35		38					44		

Date	Event	Chapter	Page
Autumn/November	New fourth Commandment		
	Windmill 'destroyed' – Snowball blamed		
Third year: winter	Struggle to rebuild windmill	7	48
End of January	Hens' eggs sold. Hens rebel		
Early spring	Snowball witch-hunt		
4 days after the 'witch-hunt'	The purge		
	'Beasts of England' banned		
A few days later	New sixth Commandment	8	52
Middle of summer	Hens admit plot to kill Napoleon		
Autumn	Structure of windmill completed		
	Battle of the Windmill		
	Pigs get drunk on whisky		
	New fifth Commandment		
Autumn	Napoleon sires 31 pigs	9	57
December	Rations reduced		
Fourth year: February	Beer for the pigs		
	'Spontaneous demonstrations'		
April	Animal Farm declared a Republic		
Middle of summer	Moses reappears		
	Boxer ill		
	Boxer taken away		
'Years passed.'	Most of original animals now dead	10	61
	'Beasts of England' sung in secret		
Early summer	Pigs walk on hind legs		
	Just one Commandment now – a new one		
	Pigs and men look the same		

Finding your way around the commentary

Each page of the commentary gives the following information:

1 A quotation from the start of each paragraph on which a comment is made, or act/scene or line numbers plus a quotation, so that you can easily locate the right place in your text.

2 A series of comments, explaining, interpreting, and drawing your attention to important incidents, characters and aspects of the text.

3 For each comment, headings to indicate the important characters, themes, and ideas dealt with in the comment.

4 For each heading, a note of the comment numbers in this guide where the previous or next comment dealing with that heading occurred.

Thus you can use this commentary section in a number of ways.

1 Turn to that part of the commentary dealing with the chapter/act you are perhaps revising for a class discussion or essay. Read through the comments in sequence, referring all the time to the text, which you should have open before you. The comments will direct your attention to all the important things of which you should take note.

2 Take a single character or topic from the list on page 20. Note the comment number next to it. Turn to that comment in this guide, where you will find the first of a number of comments on your chosen topic. Study it, and the appropriate part of your text to which it will direct you. Note the comment number in this guide where the next comment for your topic occurs and turn to it when you are ready. Thus, you can follow one topic right through your text. If you have an essay to write on a particular character or theme just follow the path through this guide and you will soon find everything you need to know!

3 A number of relevant relationships between characters and topics are listed on page 20. To follow these relationships throughout your text, turn to the comment indicated. As the previous and next comment are printed at the side of each page in the commentary, it is a simple matter to flick through the pages to find the previous or next occurrence of the relationship in which you are interested.

For example, you want to examine in depth the 'conflicts' theme of the novel. Turning to the single topic list, you will find that this theme first occurs in comment 45. On turning to comment 45 you will discover a zero (0) in the place of the previous reference (because this is the first time that it has occurred) and the number 98 for the next reference. You now turn to comment 98 and find that the previous comment number is 45 (from where you have just been looking) and that the next reference is to comment 100, and so on throughout the text.

You also wish to trace the relationship between Napoleon and the windmill throughout the novel. From the relationships list, you are directed to comment 122. This is the first time that both Napoleon and the windmill are discussed together and you will find that the next time that this happens occurs in comment 123 (the 'next' reference for both Napoleon and the windmill). On to comment 123 where you are directed to comment 124; here you will discover that two different comment numbers are given for the subject under examination – numbers 125 and 129. This is because each character and idea is traced separately as well as together and you will have to continue tracing them separately until you finally come to comment 166 – the next occasion on which both Napoleon and the windmill are discussed.

Comment number

Quote from novel

Previous appearance in guide

Character or idea under discussion

14   The two horses had . . .
What is being suggested by mentioning Mollie 'chewing at a lump of sugar'? Is it essential to her diet? What does it suggest about her nature?

5/15   The Rebellion
13/15   Mollie

Next appearance in guide

Commentary

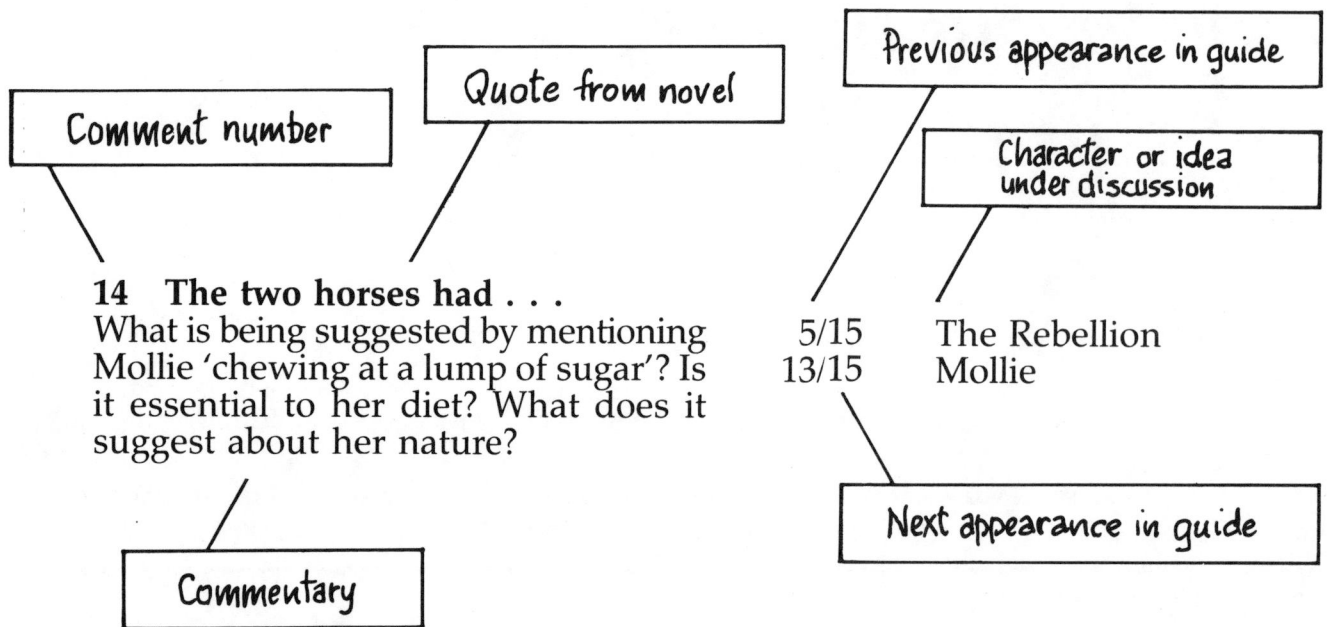

Single topics:

	Comment no:		Comment no:
The Rebellion	1	Boxer	7
Meetings	4	Clover	7
Conflicts	45	Benjamin	8
Communication	4		
The knoll	53	Moses	16
The windmill	120	Muriel	161
		Mollie	13
Old Major	3	The sheep	6
Snowball	33		
Napoleon	29	Mr Jones	1
Squealer	34	Pilkington and Frederick	95
		Mr Whymper	157

Relationships:

			Comment no:
The Rebellion	and	Napoleon	52
	and	Snowball	37
	and	Old Major	4
	and	Squealer	62
	and	Boxer	50
	and	Clover	83
Napoleon	and	Snowball	33
	and	Squealer	104
	and	The windmill	122
	and	Meetings	77
Snowball	and	Squealer	62
	and	Communication	58
	and	The windmill	122
Squealer	and	Meetings	104
	and	Communication	34
Boxer	and	Clover	7
	and	Benjamin	165

Commentary

Chapter 1

1 Mr Jones, of the . . .
Like all the human characters, Mr Jones plays a minor role in the book, although he is the motivation for the animals' revolution. Later, the threat of his return to Animal Farm helps to reinforce the pigs' authority over the other animals. He is introduced as drunk and neglectful, which provide the justification for the animals' revolt. The drunkenness which leads to Mr Jones neglecting his animals will find its mirror image at the end of the story, when the pigs exhibit exactly the same faults.

2 Mr Jones, of the . . .
Note how in this first paragraph there is no suggestion at all that Mr Jones has any redeeming features. Once he has been introduced as a drunken, neglectful farmer, the narrative immediately turns to the animals who are more worthy of our attention. Mrs Jones is introduced and dismissed in even fewer words; asleep and snoring next to her worthless husband she is, by association, equally worthless. Thus, in the first paragraph it would seem that the case for the humans has been put – and found wanting.

3 As soon as the . . .
Old Major is introduced with the notion that he had a dream important enough to be shared with all the other farm animals. From his appearance and past history it is evident that he is greatly respected by all, so that what he has to say will be regarded as highly significant. The name 'Major', having associations with the army and authority, implies some sort of seniority amongst the animals for this old boar.

4 As soon as the . . .
Notice the importance of the first meeting called by Old Major: it establishes who the characters are, the origins of the revolution and the fable nature of the story. It is significant that Old Major's vision is partly communicated in a dream. You should recognize that it is one thing to have a dream but quite another to see that dream become a reality. It is also perhaps ironic that the one animal on the farm who has apparently been well looked after should be the one who has a dream of freedom from the human's oppressive ways. Having led a life of luxury he perhaps had the time to indulge in dreams, but his legacy to the other animals was a dream which led them into even greater oppression, whilst he died peacefully in his sleep.

5 At one end of . . .
The mood of the meeting will be one of optimism and unity. Note how the mood which is exhibited by the animals at the various meetings mirrors the events in the story. There is an ironic contrast between the hopefulness of this meeting when the animals are under man's oppressive hand, and their feelings at the final meeting when they are under the oppression of their fellow animals. In one there is hope, in the other despair. Is there a lesson to be learned here?

Characters and ideas previous/next comment

0/4   The Rebellion
0/2   Mr Jones

1/30   Mr Jones

0/4   Old Major

3/11   Old Major
1/5   The Rebellion
0/17   Communication
0/5   Meetings

4/17   Meetings
4/14   The Rebellion

6 At one end of . . .

The sheep are briefly introduced along with the other animals who come to hear Old Major. Characteristically they never achieve any individual identity and merely follow whoever directs them; they always behave as one would expect sheep to behave. Be aware of how well you consider they mirror the reaction of the mass of people to events around them. Note also that they do play a crucial part in the story because of their easily led nature.

7 At one end of . . .

Boxer has two companions, Clover, a mare, and Benjamin, a donkey. Boxer and Clover have the air of being a long-married couple. As you read the story you ought to consider the extent to which they are a caricature of 'Mr and Mrs Average' who decline to use their brains, but prefer to place a blind trust in the actions and beliefs of those whom they consider, with very little real evidence, to be their betters or to know better than they do.

8 At one end of . . .

Benjamin is in direct contrast to Boxer; he is cynical and disaffected with the events and other characters of Manor Farm. However, for all his cynicism and awareness of the problems involved in making the dream a reality, and later in the pigs' actions, does he actually do anything to prevent the abuses that occur? Because of his awareness, to what extent can we accuse him of failing the Rebellion – along with other of the animals?

9 At one end of . . .

Boxer is introduced, with all the other farm animals, at the meeting called by Old Major in the barn. His appearance is closely linked with his character. What are some of the characteristics you would associate with the name, Boxer?

10 At one end of . . .

Clover is introduced with Boxer, her companion. She is established as a gentle and maternal character at the outset. Her most prominent quality is sympathy, in contrast to the callous pigs – but you must consider as you read the story the extent to which she has too narrow a view of the events happening around her: whether, perhaps, you might feel she also could have contributed more than sympathy and kindly nature to the cause of the revolution and the animals' freedom.

11 At one end of . . .

Benjamin is in contrast to Old Major who is as idealistic and theoretical as Benjamin is essentially practical and sceptical. He is given to making cryptic comments upon the events in the story. In contrast to his cynical exterior is a deep, unspoken devotion to Boxer. The unspoken nature of his affection makes it the more convincing, especially when compared with the pigs' many empty utterances of good intent.

12 The two horses had . . .

The ducklings find security with Clover in the way that other animals do later in the story when they are unhappy or insecure.

Characters and ideas previous/next comment	
0/84	The sheep
0/9	Boxer
0/10	Clover
0/11	Benjamin
7/22	Boxer
7/12	Clover
8/74	Benjamin
4/17	Old Major
10/13	Clover

13 The two horses had . . .
Consider the difference between the two mares, Mollie and Clover, both in character and appearance. Mollie is introduced as 'mincing daintily'. You should look for evidence of how she fulfils the view that the author gives of her here.

12/21	Clover
0/14	Mollie

14 The two horses had . . .
What is being suggested by mentioning Mollie 'chewing at a lump of sugar'? Is it essential to her diet? What does it suggest about her nature?

5/15	The Rebellion
13/15	Mollie

15 The two horses had . . .
Notice that Mollie's vanity is stressed here with the way she shows off her red ribbons.

14/18	The Rebellion
14/37	Mollie

16 All the animals . . .
Traditionally, a raven is a bird associated with bad luck and evil. It is most unusual that one should be kept as a pet. But note his name – Moses. In Christian art the raven is often seen as a symbol of God's bountiful nature. You should carefully note the part he plays in the story.

0/39	Moses

17 'Comrades, you have . . .'
Here is the first use of 'comrade' – a name loaded with associations to modern ears. How is Old Major using it in this context? He indicates that he is nearing the end of his life and this, coupled with an unusually long life's experience, gives his words even greater importance.

5/32	Meetings
11/18	Old Major
4/18	Communication

18 'Now, comrades, what . . .'
Having established his credentials of maturity and wisdom he describes graphically and accurately the life of an animal. Note that he uses plain simple language, repetition and short sentences that are slogan-like: 'no animal in England is free'. Why is this an effective way of communicating with the farm animals as they have been so far described in chapter 1?

15/23	The Rebellion
17/19	Communication
17/19	Old Major

19 'But is this simply . . .'
Old Major now asks questions concerning the reasons for the animals' appalling lives. This is a useful technique for a speaker, enabling him to bolster his argument with what he considers to be the right questions and the right answers. Thus the animals are not required to think for themselves, just to agree with what he says. It will be useful to compare his technique with that of Squealer later in the story.

18/20	Communication
18/20	Old Major

20 'Man is the only . . .'
Old Major has moved towards the crux of his speech – the parasitical nature of man: how man lives off the animals but gives them virtually nothing in return. Old Major shows his sympathy for the animals' lot as he gives examples of man's exploitation of the animals. There is a sharp contrast here between his view and that of the post-revolutionary pig leaders. All through the story you will see this counterbalancing of views and situations as the animals pass from one dictatorship to another.

19/22	Communication
19/22	Old Major

21 'Man is the only . . .'
References to Clover's lost foals, the stolen milk and eggs are calculated to rouse the animals' indignation and are appropriate examples of man's parasitical nature.

13/41   Clover

22 'And even the . . .'
Having carefully prepared the animals to be receptive to his words, Old Major now describes in horrific detail the deaths the animals will suffer, Boxer receiving a special mention. It is ironic that later on, Boxer assumes that such a thing can not happen with the new order.

9/36   Boxer
20/23   Old Major
20/23   Communication

23 'Is it not crystal . . .'
Old Major begins to sow the seeds for revolution but presumes that it will take several generations to achieve his idea of a Utopian society. A lot of people have had visions of a new and perfect society – some have been more successful than others in realizing it. Notice how easy the revolution will be, and how simply its results will be achieved. The animals are encouraged to work hard for the success of the revolution, but given absolutely no guidance on how to achieve it. So far Old Major has given them nothing but the substance of his dream and highlighted the injustices they are suffering – but every revolution has to start somewhere.

22/24   Old Major
22/24   Communication
18/25   The Rebellion

24 'And remember, comrades, . . .'
Old Major warns the animals against persuasive but misleading arguments. It is ironic that his first and perhaps most important warning is the one they most quickly forget; how might things have been different if they had taken his warning more to heart? The reduction of his speech to very simple slogans, so that even the dullest of animals can grasp his message, is effective but dangerous. The slogans will have to be explained and enlarged upon and in so doing are open to being changed.

23/25   Old Major
23/28   Communication

25 At this moment . . .
Already his simple slogan is being put to the test with the dogs trying to kill the rats. Blind faith in the natural goodness of 'animal' is likely to create problems, and the dogs' actions here foreshadow how Napoleon will manipulate their natural hunting and killing instincts later in the story. Old Major emphasizes the simple concept that all animals are friends and man is the only enemy. He ignores the effect of normal hardships in life such as bad weather, long cold winters or shortages of food, or that some animals naturally prey upon others. Most importantly he ignores the fact that some animals are much cleverer than others. Idealism is not enough. All the practical considerations of creating a new society have to be accounted for as well. Is this a great weakness in Old Major's dream?

24/26   Old Major
23/26   The Rebellion

26 'I have little more . . .'
Old Major warns the animals that when man is conquered the animals must be careful not to copy man's vices. All that Old Major says in this speech becomes ironic with the consequent behaviour of the pigs and some other animals. It is against this speech that the events after the Rebellion can be measured. As you read the story you should note which of the items in Old Major's list will be broken, and when.

25/27   The Rebellion
25/27   Old Major

27 'I have little more . . .'
Old Major's vision of Utopia, an ideal animal society, is based on some rather naïve and sweeping generalizations and beliefs. Is it perhaps one of his faults that he seems to see everything as a simple choice between 'black and white'?

26/28 The Rebellion
26/28 Old Major

28 Old Major cleared . . .
To conclude his speech Old Major introduces the strongly emotional appeal of the revolutionary song, 'Beasts of England', sung to him by his mother when he was very young. It describes a joyous future for the animals, stressing all the positive aspects of the new life they will lead and totally ignoring the very obvious difficulties that must face the animals if they attempt their revolution. It uses a strong and simple rhythm and rhyme pattern that makes it easily memorized and which also gives a sense of certainty and reassurance to the animals.

24/29 Communication
27/31 The Rebellion
27/31 Old Major

29 The singing of this . . .
It is important to note the way in which the singing of this song helps to unite the animals and strengthen their revolutionary zeal, and keeps an ideal fresh in their minds. When Napoleon starts to turn the revolution to his own use, he sees the danger of such a rallying point and the song is banned.

28/34 Communication
0/32 Napoleon

30 Unfortunately, the uproar . . .
Mr Jones shoots quite randomly at an imagined fox, fuelling the idea of the animals being victims of irresponsible repression – through no fault of their own. If you agree that their current situation is not of their making, as you read the story you ought to consider to what extent they bring their final misfortunes upon themselves. Is the individual always destined to suffer at the hands of those over him? Can he always hide behind the attitude that suggests a lone voice can do nothing against those in power? Do we, and the animals, get the governments that our stupidity deserves?

2/36 Mr Jones

Chapter 2

31 Three nights later . . .
Old Major dies, peacefully, and is buried decently compared with the way that other animals are slaughtered. His burial near the orchard, suggesting both final peace and a fruitful growth of his ideas, is a nice image upon which to leave him. However, the idea that he would not have been slaughtered by Farmer Jones, for profit, seems rather strange! His words have sown the seed of revolution in the animals' minds but to what extent has he failed them by not presenting them with the realities of a revolution?

28/35 The Rebellion
28/32 Old Major

32 This was early . . .
At once the pigs begin to teach and organize the animals, preparing the way for their later supremacy. Napoleon is introduced, with Snowball, immediately after the death of Old Major. Towards the bottom of the page Squealer is introduced, which gives us the four dominant pigs for comparison at the very beginning of the Rebellion. Note the names of these

17/36 Meetings
29/33 Napoleon
31/135 Old Major

four pigs and what they imply. Old Major, one of the 'old school', is reliable, predictable, an idealist who was out of touch with the real world – as is suggested by the easy life he led at the farm. Napoleon is a fierce and determined pig, named after one of Europe's most famous revolutionaries who turned a popular uprising into a dictatorship.

33 This was early . . . .
The name Snowball foreshadows how he melts away before the onslaught of Napoleon's brutality. What other associations does the name Snowball have? His qualities are clearly set against Napoleon's for comparison.

32/51	Napoleon
0/37	Snowball

34 This was early . . .
The name Squealer has several associations. His sly and underhand ways, his manipulation of the other animals are all aspects of his character which will be demonstrated in the story. Note how, even before the Rebellion, he is said to be able to turn 'black into white'.

29/39	Communication
0/62	Squealer

35 These three had . . .
Napoleon and the other two leading pigs translate Old Major's vision into a workable system, but encounter difficulties in getting across theories to the animals. You should consider why these difficulties arise. Note the stupidity, self-interest and apathy displayed by the various animals.

31/37	The Rebellion

36 These three had . . .
Mr Jones is always asleep – in more ways than one – when the animals hold their secret meetings. Compare the way that Jones is spoken of here, with the way Boxer and others speak of Napoleon later on.

32/42	Meetings
22/41	Boxer
30/43	Mr Jones

37 'No,' said Snowball . . .
Snowball is probably the brains behind the working out of the principle of Animalism, and with the other pigs tries to convey these ideas to the rest of the animals. Consider the importance of what Snowball says to Mollie; ribbons are perhaps the most useless thing an animal can have or desire yet Mollie seems to equate their importance with oats and hay. Snowball's clear idea of what is important is revealed here, his firmness and austere attitude are clearly established.

35/38	The Rebellion
33/50	Snowball
15/38	Mollie

38 Mollie agreed, but . . .
The reader can see that Mollie is not the stuff from which revolutions are made! By contrast, what does this suggest about the qualities necessary for any hope of a successful change for better in society?

37/40	The Rebellion
37/55	Mollie

39 The pigs had an . . .
Moses the raven was absent during Old Major's assembly. He is later introduced and established as Jones's special pet. Consider the implications of such a simplistic notion of a life hereafter which Moses presents: why should we worry about things now when such a wonderful life after death awaits us? The author is using Moses as a vehicle to criticize the established churches and their view of what is more important to man in the long term: this world or the next. Much as the pigs ridicule Moses' ideas, do watch for how they later turn them to their advantage.

34/42	Communication
16/40	Moses

40 The pigs had an . . .
What is the significance of Moses' claim that animals go to 'Sugarcandy Mountain' when they die? Sugar-candy is not particularly good for animals and it suggests sweets given to children perhaps as a reward, or as a bribe. Is this what religion should be about?

38/42	The Rebellion
39/43	Moses

---

41 Their most faithful . . .
The respect which the other animals give to Boxer and Clover is of great assistance in getting the pigs' ideas accepted, once these two have taken them to heart. Unfortunately, they do not have the intelligence or wit to think for themselves – much to their own loss later in the story. Are we to assume that those of great physical strength are always incapable of intelligent thought?

36/50	Boxer
21/83	Clover

---

42 Their most faithful . . .
Be aware of the unifying and exciting effect of secret meetings on the animals. Something like a conditioning process is taking place, with the repetition of revolutionary principles and the singing of the stirring 'Beasts of England'. The reinforcement of future hopes and the rallying effect of its optimistic theme keep the animals keyed up, and it plays a part in their readiness to rebel when driven to do so by Mr Jones.

39/58	Communication
36/44	Meetings
40/43	The Rebellion

---

43 Now, as it turned . . .
The downfall of Mr Jones, disheartened after a lawsuit and befuddled by drink, foreshadows the scheming and drinking of Napoleon and the other pigs. Just as Mr Jones's men were idle and dishonest, so too will become the pigs who support Napoleon. Under Mr Jones the animals are underfed, under Napoleon their fate will be rather worse. The disreputable way in which Moses lives, feeding on crusts of bread soaked in beer is a measure of the decadence of Mr Jones.

42/45	The Rebellion
40/47	Moses
36/44	Mr Jones

---

44 June came and . . .
Ironically, the 'harvest' that Mr Jones has cultivated is ready for reaping in more ways than one. He triggers off the revolution by neglecting the animals while getting drunk in Willingdon and ignoring the feeding of his animals once too often. With the combination of factors, revolution becomes inevitable and can clearly be seen to be justified – in spite of what happens later. However, note that although the secret meetings undoubtedly helped put the animals in the right frame of mind to rebel, the revolution actually happens as a result of two very basic 'human' drives: anger and hunger.

42/60	Meetings
43/48	Mr Jones

---

45 June came and . . .
Compare the mood of this skirmish with the intense feelings of later battles. No one is hurt and the humans look silly rather than tragic as they take to their heels.

0/98	Conflicts
43/46	The Rebellion

---

46 Mrs Jones looked . . .
The only mention of Mrs Jones is when she throws a few possessions in a bag and hurries away from the farm. Her only contribution is in leaving her clothes, later to be worn by Napoleon's favourite sow.

45/48	The Rebellion

---

47 Mrs Jones looked . . .

As Moses to an extent represents the church, his living with Jones suggests that the church was on the side of the oppressors. Do retain a balance when interpreting this 'fable'. Most certainly, horrific crimes have been committed by men in the name of religion, as well as in the name of freedom, equality and justice; all men are not evil, good, equal or free in the same way or measure.

43/235   Moses

48 Mrs Jones looked . . .

Jones is expelled by the united animals quickly and easily. Compared with what comes later, the overthrow of Jones the tyrant is simple and straight-forward, more so than Old Major had ever supposed possible. It will now be seen whether his view of life after the Rebellion is quite so rosy a picture as he painted!

46/50   The Rebellion
44/49   Mr Jones

49 For the first few . . .

All the cruel and humiliating means by which Jones held the animals in submission, for example nose-rings and dog chains, are easy to identify. You should keep this in mind as the story develops and consider how the pigs keep the animals enslaved without such means. Be aware that psycho-logical chains can be as effective as physical ones. You should try to identify the fears and other emotions that the pigs exploit to gain power over the other animals.

48/94   Mr Jones

50 'Ribbons,' he said . . .

Snowball has once before been critical of ribbons and the vanities that go with them – can you remember when? Here, he develops his ideas more fully, declaring that they are the mark of the hated humans and that therefore all animals should go naked. Note how suddenly some animals are making rules that others will have to obey. There has been no discussion, merely an issued decree. As a result, Boxer decides to give up his straw hat – not worn in vanity, but to keep away flies in summer – as a demonstration of wholehearted support of the animals' uprising. It is typical of Boxer's lack of self-esteem that he equates his working hat with Mollie's silly ribbons, after Snowball's comments. This is an early indication of his naïvety and self-sacrifice. But note that whilst his sacrifice hurts only him, the rash abandoning of good sense is a stark contrast to the calculating way in which the pigs will go about their work. Should we admire Boxer for his attitude?

48/52   The Rebellion
41/56   Boxer
37/51   Snowball

51 In a very little while . . .

It was Snowball who led the animals in their destruction of the hated symbols of oppression. Notice how Napoleon assumes the role of provider when he organizes the distribution of food to the animals; which action are the animals more likely to remember? Could you give reasons why? Napoleon takes an early lead in establishing a position which he never loses, although at first his manipulation of the situation is quite low-key.

33/52   Napoleon
50/54   Snowball

52 In a very little while . . .

Consider the implications of Napoleon as a provider immediately after the revolution. There was no wild raid on the store of food as one might have expected after such an exciting occasion, but rather a careful allocation of

50/53   The Rebellion
51/54   Napoleon

corn and biscuits, controlled by Napoleon and totally lacking in any sort of spontaneous generosity or emotion. Already he is establishing himself in a position of power, controlling the allocation and distribution of the key product: food. What impression here do we gain of Napoleon's motives?

53 But they woke at . . .
The animals are joyful as, from the top of the knoll, they view the farm they now control. There is a nice structural counterbalance to this scene later in the story when the knoll is the setting for their confessions and executions. The differences between the two scenes are also reflected in the bodily movements of the animals – it would be a useful exercise to look at those words which describe the scenes and pick out those which convey the difference in atmosphere.

0/120   The knoll
52/55   The Rebellion

54 Then they filed . . .
Snowball and Napoleon take the lead going into the farmhouse. Consider how much in character this is for Snowball in the light of what comes later, but not so for Napoleon, who more and more becomes the power behind the scene with others carrying out his orders.

52/57   Napoleon
51/58   Snowball

55 Then they filed . . .
Yet again Mollie has to be cautioned about her liking for ribbons. The sharp contrast between Mollie's ribbons and the hams being reverently taken out for burial serves to highlight the enormous gulf between the attitudes and hopes of the various animals who take part in the revolution.

53/56   The Rebellion
38/73   Mollie

56 Then they filed . . .
Note the concern and emotion represented in the hams that were taken out for burial and Boxer kicking in the barrel of beer which represented the cause of so much of their past suffering. Keep this scene in mind when later in the story we see how the pigs make use of Jones's house, particularly in their gross appetite for food and drink.

55/58   The Rebellion
50/72   Boxer

57 Then they filed . . .
The agreement that no animal should ever live in the farmhouse is yet another of the many resolutions which will be ignored or altered. Napoleon, presumably, had no intention of keeping his word.

54/59   Napoleon

58 The pigs now . . .
Consider the significance of the stress that Snowball lays on literacy. How might life for the animals have been different if they could have learned to read and write? Do you think there was any real desire on Napoleon's part for all the animals to become literate? Bear in mind that in any modern society, a literate, concerned and involved population is a key to democracy. When a large section of the community is illiterate or only barely literate, so that they find keeping up with the flow of words produced by politicians too much of an effort, then democratic institutions face real danger from ambitious men.

42/59   Communication
56/60   The Rebellion
54/59   Snowball

59 The pigs now . . .
Napoleon leads the way to the Manor Farm gate, but it is Snowball who paints in the name Animal Farm. It is noticeable that although Napoleon gives the orders it is Snowball who possesses the skill to write.

58/60	Communication
57/67	Napoleon
58/61	Snowball

60 The pigs now . . .
The next meeting is called by Snowball and Napoleon to introduce more revolutionary ideas: reading and the concepts of Animalism. At this stage the two leaders work together in apparent harmony, or do you think that Napoleon is merely biding his time?

59/62	Communication
44/76	Meetings
58/61	The Rebellion

61 The pigs now . . .
Snowball shows himself to be the most intellectual of the animals by actually writing the Seven Commandments and, we suspect, taking the major part in composing them. Thus he establishes the apparently firm foundation for the post-revolution life of Animal Farm. It is important that you are aware of when and how these Commandments are gradually changed as the pigs gain more power, and the results of the changes on the animals' lives. You should also consider what are the weaknesses in their society that enable the pigs to distort the Commandments out of all recognition from their original meaning and purpose.

60/62	The Rebellion
59/62	Snowball

62 The pigs now . . .
Squealer, with Snowball doing the actual writing, helps to establish the Seven Commandments on the big barn wall. It will not be that long before Squealer is no longer just holding the paintpot but actually doing the writing; he will alter the Commandments to fit in with whatever the pigs regard as helpful to them at the time.

60/63	The Rebellion
60/63	Communication
59/63	Snowball
34/79	Squealer

63 The pigs now . . .
With all the best intentions Snowball summarizes the ideas of Animalism into Seven Commandments and writes them on the barn wall for all to read and observe as 'an unalterable law by which all animals on Animal Farm must live for ever after'. Why is this ironic, and sad? The Seven Commandments were intended as guidelines and a safeguard for the constitution of Animal Farm, in fact they were exploited and used to manipulate the working animals. Is the key to their failure to safeguard the animals' interests to be found in their inability to learn to read and their short memories?

62/67	Snowball
62/64	The Rebellion
62/64	Communication

64 The pigs now . . .
The revolutionary ideals of Old Major find their expression in the Seven Commandments. Is it only the desire of the pigs to tell the other animals 'as much as it is good for them to know' that inspires them to write the Commandments in this way? As each Commandment is successively betrayed we can see the increasing corruption of the original ideal that started the revolution. You also ought to consider the parallel here between the Seven Commandments and the Ten Commandments that hold such a central position in Christian belief. Do you think the author is suggesting that, just as the pigs of Animal Farm interpret their Commandments to suit the moment, so man does the same thing with his?

63/65	The Rebellion
63/65	Communication

65 It was very . . .
There is a gulf opening between 'the cleverer ones' and the other animals in their understanding and knowledge of the Seven Commandments. One of the key points of *Animal Farm* is that the language of governments is something remote from the average man and his spoken language. Snowball did his best to attempt to simplify the system of Animalism in the Seven Commandments and with various slogans, but the simplification of language is insufficient if the animals are not literate, too busy with other matters, cynical, or just uninterested in their own welfare – though they obviously do not see it in this light!

| 64/66 | The Rebellion |
| 64/75 | Communication |

66 THE SEVEN COMMANDMENTS . . .
As you read the story you should keep careful note of how these Commandments are gradually changed, deleted and finally abolished completely. Their gradual erosion marks the watering down of Old Major's high ideals and the descent of the animals to a life far worse than that experienced under Jones.

| 65/68 | The Rebellion |

67 'Now, comrades,' said . . .
Snowball here shows his practical nature and grasp of what should be essential considerations. Contrast his attitude and concerns with that of Napoleon three paragraphs on – Napoleon has more important things with which to concern himself.

| 59/68 | Napoleon |
| 63/75 | Snowball |

68 'Jones used sometimes . . .'
There is a mention of Jones mixing surplus milk in the hens' mash. This is not a practice that Napoleon will follow, and if you check the final chapter you will see just how much worse life for the animals becomes under Napoleon.

| 66/69 | The Rebellion |
| 67/69 | Napoleon |

69 So the animals . . .
The suspicious disappearance of the milk is prefaced by Napoleon's sly and hypocritical encouragement of the animals to attend to the harvest, and we have the first hint of Napoleon's greed. His method of operation is beginning to be made clear to the reader, even if the animals fail to realize what is going on.

| 68/70 | The Rebellion |
| 68/77 | Napoleon |

70 So the animals . . .
The animals leave for the hayfield, inspired by the new life that is opening before them. Sadly, this new idea that could have benefited them so much is already under attack; it is an ominous sign for the future.

| 69/71 | The Rebellion |

Chapter 3

71 How they toiled . . .
In these introductory paragraphs we see some measure of how the revolution might have worked. Almost every animal gave of its best,

| 70/72 | The Rebellion |

unselfishly and willingly. There was total cooperation and not a grain was stolen. As yet, there is nothing sinister in the fact that they worked under the direction of the pigs. You should be aware that the animals work just as hard now, if not more so, than they ever do under Napoleon's oppressive style of leadership. You need to consider Napoleon's motives in the way he treats the animals. When he gains power he will want to keep it, but being afraid of losing his power he will become oppressive and brutal. Does power always corrupt its holder? You might like to discuss with friends what checks and balances society should provide to keep those in power under some sort of control.

72 All through that . . .
Boxer is essential to the success of the farm; he takes such a pride in achievement that he earns the respect of all. However, allied to these good qualities is a flaw; his view of events is limited to simple slogans. By limiting himself in this way he effectively becomes the willing tool (slave would not be too strong a word) of Napoleon's corrupt ambitions to take complete control of the farm.

71/75   The Rebellion
56/83   Boxer

73 But everyone worked . . .
Consider how lazy and deceitful Mollie is when work needs to be done. Throughout she is a passenger of, if not a positive hindrance to, the new society. The author is pointing to an example of an individual who is flawed and who would be useless no matter what social system was adopted. The cat is another example of a parasite, feeding on the efforts of others and contributing nothing himself.

55/108   Mollie

74 But everyone worked . . .
Benjamin stubbornly remains unmoved by the revolution in a way that suggests that he has low expectations of the new Animal Farm, unlike Boxer who expects so much and receives so little. Is Benjamin wiser than the other animals in his view of the future, or he is yet another reason why the revolution fails—as indeed it does in terms of the Seven Commandments and Old Major's dream? It is perhaps not unreasonable that he should take a very realistic, even cynical view of events, but is he right to stand back from trying to influence them? One often hears the cry 'I'm only one person, I can't do anything!'—yet individuals like Napoleon allow no such defeatist ideas to stand in their way!

11/102   Benjamin

75 On Sundays there . . .
National anthems and flags ought to uplift and inspire, though they can be put to very different purposes. You need to be aware of how these symbols are used, and abused, at Animal Farm, What do the 'hoof' and 'horn' caricature from the flag of Russia?

65/79   Communication
72/83   The Rebellion
67/77   Snowball

76 On Sundays there . . .
What is the importance of the regular Sunday meeting for the animals? What is the difference between the participation of the animals and that of the pigs? Notice the energetic and positive mood of these Sunday meetings, compared with what comes later.

60/77   Meetings

	Characters and ideas previous/next comment	

77 On Sundays there . . .

The two leaders openly dispute ideas in a way that never happens after Snowball leaves the farm. Note, however, that the disagreements are not constructive and useful, but disagreement purely because the point of view was that of someone else. This is sometimes referred to as 'confrontation politics' and you might like to consider how well such politics serve the mass of the population; you also might like to consider whether you ever see examples of it in our own political system. However, for all their drawbacks the open debates on policy and planning did take place at the beginning whereas later in the story they no longer occur. Any open system of government, however self-centred and power-seeking, is probably better than one where such openness is not possible. What lessons were learned from these debates with Snowball by Napoleon, do you suppose?

76/109	Meetings
69/78	Napoleon
75/78	Snowball

78 The pigs had . . .

The role of Napoleon at this stage is not always clear, but Snowball is always busy with schemes that benefit the animals.

77/79	Snowball
77/87	Napoleon

79 The pigs had . . .

What do you think of the various committees that Snowball formed, especially bearing in mind the animals with which they dealt? To what extent do you think the author is commenting on the great gulf that lies between Snowball's ideals and the other animals' simple hopes? Squealer seemed to have a much better understanding of the audience with which he was dealing; certainly his comment later that 'surely none of you want Jones back' was a very effective line of communication and persuasion.

75/80	Communication
78/85	Snowball
62/90	Squealer

80 The pigs had . . .

There is a nice ironic touch here which gives a good example of the pigs' 'doubletalk' and the extent to which they should be believed. It is the cat, always absent when there is work to be done, who tells the sparrows 'that all animals are now comrades', and they believe him about as much as the other animals ought to believe Napoleon.

79/81	Communication

81 The reading and . . .

The news that almost every animal on the farm was literate to some degree should give great satisfaction, but the ability to read is not in itself sufficient. If what we read adds nothing to our knowledge and understanding and is garbled and worthless, then what is the value of being literate?

80/82	Communication

82 As for the pigs, . . .

In this catalogue of who can read, how well, and to what uses they put their reading, we see a savage satire on our own society, as well as that of Animal Farm. The pigs learn well and make the most of their learning, benefiting themselves to the exclusion of all others. The dogs stunted their own growth by refusing to broaden their reading beyond what they easily understood. Muriel the goat used a garbage heap as the source of her reading. Benjamin simply refused to use his ability – an almost criminal waste of talent. Clover and Boxer tried, but failed. Mollie could consider nothing more than her own ridiculous vanity. Look around your own circle of acquaintances; could you identify some of these characters?

81/83	Communication

83 As for the pigs, . . .
Clover shows herself to be a little more intelligent than Boxer, but is not as strong as he is physically. From time to time she shows slightly more perception than he does of the events at Animal Farm but not enough to see through the double-dealing of the power-hungry pigs. Boxer and Clover's difficulties in mastering the simple concept of the alphabet leads them to be content with infrequent use of it. Can you see that this is to be an omen for the animals' downfall?

82/85	Communication
72/106	Boxer
41/113	Clover
75/86	The Rebellion

84 None of the . . .
For the first part of the story the sheep are not referred to individually, or differentiated from the other farm animals. Here they are referred to as some of 'the stupider animals'. You might like to consider how just this description of them turns out to be.

| 6/85 | The sheep |

85 None of the . . .
Undeterred by the failure of some animals to learn to read and write adequately Snowball cleverly adapts the principles of Animalism to a clear expression that the dimmest animal can understand: 'Four legs good, two legs bad'. He shows the clarity of his thinking in his definition to the birds of man's hand as the instrument with which he does his mischief. Tragically, the sheep take this simplification too much to heart and later will use its mindless repetition to thwart Snowball's good intentions.

83/86	Communication
79/87	Snowball
84/86	The sheep

86 The birds did . . .
What is the significance of the value Snowball attaches to the humbler animals understanding the essential principle of Animalism? Perhaps he recognizes the great threat their ignorance could pose to the revolution. Do you understand what that threat might be? (The sheep will later give a good example of it!) Does Snowball feel that the threat to the animals is less likely to be external, that is from the humans, than internal, that is from some of their fellow animals?

85/88	Communication
83/87	The Rebellion
85/118	The sheep

87 Napoleon took no . . .
The dogs are introduced as puppies, when Napoleon isolates and 'educates' them away from all other influences. Dictators are not the only people who recognize the value of training in childhood. Any nation's future lies in the hands of its children, and the better educated – in its widest sense – that they are, the better for the nation. However, we must not forget that Napoleon's plans for the puppies had very little to do with education, but more with indoctrination. It will be interesting to compare the puppyhood of the dogs with the élitist upbringing of the young pigs later on.

86/89	The Rebellion
85/88	Snowball
78/88	Napoleon

88 Napoleon took no . . .
The puppies will become Napoleon's bodyguard and eventually chase Snowball from the farm. Could it be that Napoleon has this in mind from the start of their upbringing, which coincides with his split with Snowball and Snowball's increasing popularity with the other animals? The two forms of education are placed side by side for comparison: Napoleon's conditioning of the dogs and Snowball's literacy classes. Which would you say was the more successful, and why? In answering this question do distinguish between the objectives of the two forms of education, the animals they were working with and the conditions under which the education took place.

86/90	Communication
87/89	Snowball
87/89	Napoleon

Characters and ideas previous/next comment

89 The mystery of . . .
The mystery of the disappearing milk is explained. Can you remember how it was used in Jones's time? Already we see a clear indication of the way events are moving. What is interesting is the way in which Snowball participates in this unfairness. Note also the importance of Snowball's agreement to the selfish act of keeping the windfall apples for the pigs' use. Is this in Snowball's character as it is portrayed, in the same way that it is an essential part of Napoleon's character?

90 'Comrades!' he cried. . . .
At one time, the animals' use of the word 'comrades' had a definite suggestion to it that all were actually equal. Here, it is used by Squealer to conceal the fact that they are no longer equal–can you see how? With the pigs consuming the milk and apples instead of sharing equally, Squealer is used as a 'front man' to lie to and frighten the other animals, while both Napoleon and Snowball stay in the background. The ease with which the animals are duped over something as basic as food is an indicator of their acceptance of the pigs' assumption of power.

91 'Comrades!' he cried. . . .
From being a founder-member of the revolution until the end of the story, it is Squealer who persuades and threatens the animals into complying with the pigs' rulings. Be aware of how he accomplishes this essential task. Here he gives plausible-sounding reasons for the pigs' assumption of privilege. If the animals had been a little less in awe of 'brainwork' in others and used their own brains more they would have seen through his reasons which were devoid of everything except artfulness. Should his 'reasons' not be convincing enough he ends with what is to be a recurring threat, 'who wants to see Jones back?' Events are still fresh enough in the animals' minds, and the pigs' excesses not sufficiently obvious yet, for this to be a considerable threat to the animals. Later, however, this threat will lose its force, and will be replaced by a sinister growl from the dogs to punctuate and emphasize his propaganda.

92 Now if there . . .
What makes the pigs' selfishness so much more unbearable is the evil that accompanies it. The indignation felt by the reader is not shared by the animals, whose opinions are swayed, more than anything else, by the implied threat of Jones's return. After all, it turns out to be true that the pigs do keep away Jones!

Chapter 4

93 By the late . . .
Be aware of how closely the two leaders work together at first. Here they seek to incite the animals on neighbouring farms to revolution.

Characters and ideas previous/next comment	
87/90	The Rebellion
88/93	Snowball
88/93	Napoleon
88/91	Communication
89/92	The Rebellion
79/91	Squealer
90/96	Communication
90/104	Squealer
90/97	The Rebellion
89/104	Napoleon
89/100	Snowball

94 Most of this . . .

Mr Jones is portrayed as weak and slightly ridiculous: as the pub bore who fails to gain sympathy from his neighbours. He is always an uninteresting character and although unpleasant, never comes alive for the reader in the way that the main animal characters do. None of the humans in the story is given a really major part to play – they are caricatures of the less pleasant types of man who thereby enable the animals to imitate and distort their worst failings.

95 Most of this . . .

Mr Pilkington of Foxwood and Mr Frederick of Pinchfield are introduced together, as neighbouring farmers who do not get on with each other, nor particularly well with the deposed Jones. Their initial role is that of a threat to Animal Farm, and to provide more justification for the revolution in the first place – as indeed do all the unattractive human characters. As neighbouring farmers they had an interest in seeing that the revolution did not succeed; however, being on bad terms with each other they failed to grasp the opportunity that joint action could have provided. Note how later on Napoleon will make use of their enmity for each other for his own gain.

96 Nevertheless, they were . . .

Notice the frightening nature of the rumours put about by Pilkington and Frederick. Do you suppose these stories were consciously invented by the two men, or do you think that they half believed them to be true? Whatever their beliefs, there is a certain irony in the stories in that to an extent they do predict some of the events that will happen. Which of their stories eventually have an element of truth in them?

97 However, these stories . . .

The discontent which spread from Animal Farm had a worrying effect on the local farmers, who acted with some brutality to suppress any possibility of revolution happening on their farms. However, they will eventually learn to live and trade with, and then enjoy the company of the revolutionaries – especially when they realize that the pigs, in making the revolution their own, have become just like men. Notice the subversive potential of 'Beasts of England', in the way the song is used among animals on neighbouring farms, accompanied by acts of destruction. It acts as a rallying call and reminder of Old Major's ideals, so you can see that eventually Napoleon will find it just as dangerous as the farmers do now.

98 Early in October, . . .

At last we see Jones's attempts to recapture the farm. Once more the humans are dispatched relatively easily, albeit at some cost to the animals. The dispatching of Jones, his men and their guns, perhaps signals that such obvious threats are easier to deal with than is the manipulation of language and emotion, both of which will be a greater threat to the animals' freedom.

99 Early in October, . . .

Pilkington and Frederick allowed their men to help Jones attempt to regain his farm, but did not go themselves. Thus, they could not be identified with Jones as enemies of the animals. Would you say that there was an equal degree of cowardice and self-interest in their actions? If Jones succeeded, they could say they helped him, but if he failed they could disown him.

Characters and ideas
previous/next comment

49/98	Mr Jones
0/96	Pilkington and Frederick
91/97	Communication
95/99	Pilkington and Frederick
92/109	The Rebellion
96/98	Communication
97/103	Communication
45/100	Conflicts
94/99	Mr Jones
98/141	Mr Jones
96/159	Pilkington and Frederick

Certainly, at the end of the story they manage to be on friendly terms with Napoleon and the pigs. 'Nothing succeeds like success': what kind of success are they interested in?

100 This had long . . .
It is plain that Snowball's mastering of military strategy, brilliant leadership and personal courage at the Battle of the Cowshed is crucial. Without this, the victory all the animals had worked for would have been lost. However, the very brilliance of Snowball's planning and victory sowed the seeds of his future expulsion by Napoleon. Why do you think this is so?

98/101	Conflicts
93/103	Snowball

101 This had long . . .
Note the importance of the Battle of the Cowshed, as the success is crucial when one considers what would have happened if the humans had won.

100/102	Conflicts

102 As the human . . .
Benjamin is in the front line of attack at the Battle of the Cowshed. With him, actions always speak louder than words, unlike the pigs whose words promise what they never actually deliver. Despite his cynicism, when the animals are under a direct and concrete threat he is prepared to act with them. Why does he not act when faced by the more sinister, but less obvious, threat posed by Napoleon?

101/104	Conflicts
74/165	Benjamin

103 The men gave . . .
The wounded Snowball demonstrates to everyone his bravery by attacking Jones. Even with this concrete example of Snowball's sterling worth note how easily the animals will be misled by propaganda later on.

98/105	Communication
100/105	Snowball

104 The men gave . . .
Squealer, like Napoleon, is involved at the rear of the Battle of the Cowshed, in contrast to Snowball and Boxer!

102/105	Conflicts
93/105	Napoleon
91/139	Squealer

105 The men gave . . .
The names of both Napoleon and Squealer are conspicuous by their absence throughout the battle and its aftermath. There is some mention of 'the rest of the pigs' and we might suppose these two are included – what do you think and can you justify your opinions on the matter? However, it is Snowball who is the hero of the hour and he is justly decorated. You should keep the events of the Battle in mind for Napoleon will see to it that, in the course of time, history gets rewritten and Snowball's glorious moment will be described quite differently. This is often a deceit which dictators feel necessary to practise. Can you think why?

104/106	Conflicts
104/116	Napoleon
103/107	Snowball
103/116	Communication

106 The men gave . . .
We see here an indication of Boxer's power, already suggested when he destroyed the beer-barrel with one kick earlier in the story. How different things might have been if the use of his strength had been differently guided – with more intelligent use of it or with more enlightened self-interest on his part. His part in the Battle, particularly in knocking out the stable-lad, led to the retreat of Jones's men.

105/107	Conflicts
83/107	Boxer

107 'He is dead,' . . .
Boxer's compassion for the stable-lad and his worry about the others' opinion of his action give us an insight into his character and priorities. From his words it would seem that he had no desire to kill or maim, merely to frighten. In contrast, be aware of Snowball's brisk, no-nonsense attitude to casualties of the Battle of the Cowshed. He has his sights set on a particular goal and is not deflected by other considerations. Is this a good quality in a leader? Note the maxims that Snowball utters from time to time, for example 'The only good human being is a dead one'. They provide an insight into the way his mind works. Can you remember when he said, 'All animals should go naked'?

106/108	Conflicts
106/142	Boxer
105/110	Snowball

108 Mollie was in . . .
Mollie takes no useful part in the Battle of the Cowshed. How much is her flight due to fear, or to a lack of identification with the other animals? Has she been so long made a pet of by Jones that she is no longer really a farm animal? Can you think of another farm animal of which the same could be said?

107/109	Conflicts
73/112	Mollie

109 The animals had . . .
The two major battles, of the Cowshed and the Windmill, come at crucial moments for the animals. Here, led by Snowball, the animals are coordinated and united in their defence of Animal Farm. They are proud and dignified in victory. They need no reassurances and make their own decisions as to whom honours should be awarded. After the Battle of the Windmill they will be sorrowful and weary, needing to be reassured by Squealer. The celebrations will be carefully contrived with songs, speeches and firings of the gun – followed by the drunken debauch of the pigs.

108/111	Conflicts
77/116	Meetings
97/110	The Rebellion

110 The animals decided . . .
Consider the importance of Snowball's decoration and the way in which the memory of it will become distorted and degraded, in a way that parallels what happened to all the finer qualities of the animals after the Rebellion. The giving of horse-brass medals has a certain irony, reminding us of when Jones would use these same brasses to decorate his horses. Now, they also serve to link Snowball and Boxer as the brains and brawn of the battle.

109/115	The Rebellion
107/116	Snowball

111 There was much . . .
Mr Jones's gun is retained as a trophy, to become a reminder of past glories in the days to follow. Increasingly this will become a sad reminder of unfulfilled hopes and promises.

109/206	Conflicts

Chapter 5

112 As winter drew . . .
Mollie could be said to represent one of the less useful members of any society; she is too self-absorbed to be of any use to anyone.

108/113	Mollie

113 'Mollie,' she said, . . .
Clover shows a certain maternal wisdom in noting Mollie's defection. Motherlike, she is discreet enough not to tell the others what she has discovered. There is about Clover's portrayal something of the idealized feeling that many people have for their country.

83/152 Clover
112/114 Mollie

114 'He didn't! I . . .'
Mollie has utilized her only assets, her appearance and servile nature, in the way that suits her best. Unlike Snowball, she is soon forgotten for the nonentity that she was.

113/0 Mollie

115 A thought struck . . .
Mollie's lack of character is seen in her passion for sugar and coloured ribbon. By linking Mollie with such luxuries, just as beer and Jones are linked, and the pigs are associated with whisky and an excessive amount of food, the author implies fundamental flaws in these characters. Conversely, frugality and self-sacrifice, as with Boxer, tell of moral strength.

110/121 The Rebellion

116 In January there . . .
What is the significance of the pigs' new role? Signs of social change and division are becoming apparent. The pigs now decide all questions of farm policy. At the moment their decisions have to be agreed by a majority vote of all the animals – watch out for how soon this only check on the pigs' power will be discarded as unnecessary. There is a widening gulf of opinion between Snowball and Napoleon which shows up at the meetings more clearly than at other times in the life of the farm. Snowball wins popularity with 'his brilliant speeches' and clever schemes. However, it is interesting to note that these qualities do nothing to warn him of the danger he is in from Napoleon.

109/118 Meetings
110/117 Snowball
105/125 Communication
105/117 Napoleon

117 In January there . . .
Note the differences in leadership styles between Snowball and Napoleon. Snowball has practical vision and ingenuity at educating himself and producing clever schemes that would benefit everyone. He wins the hearts of the animals but fails to get their votes. Napoleon engages his time criticizing Snowball's plans and making sure that the majority vote goes his way – the sheep are crucial here.

116/118 Napoleon
116/118 Snowball

118 In January there . . .
The mindless and manipulated response of the sheep has a disastrous effect on the attempt of the animals to win their freedom from oppression. Napoleon uses them to disrupt Snowball's speeches and later on to shout down any protester who is in opposition to him. In refusing to think for themselves and allowing themselves to be led to mindless and disruptive tactics at meetings, the sheep most certainly contribute in a major way to Napoleon's rise to power and their own eventual oppression. What sort of people would you say they represent in modern society?

86/138 The sheep
116/119 Meetings
117/119 Snowball
117/119 Napoleon

119 In January there . . .
There is a widening rift between Snowball and Napoleon both personally and in style of leadership. The meetings in the big barn highlight this process. The gaining of power by Napoleon is all behind the scenes, and

118/128 Meetings
118/122 Napoleon
118/122 Snowball

thus more effective. Napoleon's cunning and deceit are gradually being revealed and a threat to Snowball becomes apparent.

120 In the long . . .

You should take note of the events that occur on the knoll. After the revolution the animals stood there in joy looking out over the farm they controlled. Now it is to become the site of a major construction, the windmill, which will benefit every animal on the farm. Despite the glories associated with the knoll, note what it and the windmill will be used for later in the story.

53/121	The knoll
0/121	The windmill

121 In the long . . .

The knoll is obviously the best place to site the windmill. It is also the highest point from which to view Animal Farm, and the most visible landmark to the neighbouring farmers. It is a symbol of the pride felt by the animals in their achievements.

120/188	The knoll
115/122	The Rebellion
120/122	The windmill

122 Within a few . . .

The windmill that Snowball plans to take the drudgery out of the animals' lives is a tribute to his technical ingenuity in planning such an enterprise. Note the reaction of the animals to Snowball's intelligence – including Napoleon's. Is this why Snowball had to be disposed of? Could Napoleon no longer accept this threat to his leadership? Napoleon's crude rejection of the plans by urinating over them tells us more about him than anything he has said so far. It is a savage comment both on the nature of Napoleon's leadership and on the way that intellectuals are often treated by oppressive dictatorships.

121/126	The Rebellion
121/123	The windmill
119/123	Napoleon
119/123	Snowball

123 The whole farm . . .

Snowball gives a realistic appraisal of the chances of building the windmill. You should note how it compares with Napoleon's wild predictions and bizarre excuses for failure later in the story.

122/124	The windmill
122/124	Napoleon
122/124	Snowball

124 The whole farm . . .

The windmill is so important that the key election between Snowball and Napoleon is based on its possible future. It is vital because such machinery would alter the whole structure of the farm's economic life. The way in which this new power would be used for the good of the animals highlights the difference between Snowball and Napoleon.

123/129	The windmill
123/125	Napoleon
123/125	Snowball

125 The whole farm . . .

Compare the two election slogans of Snowball and Napoleon with what actually happens. Notice what Snowball visualizes as the animals' society in the future. How different life would have been if Snowball had won the election and stayed in power – or would it? What evidence is there so far that Snowball was not averse to helping himself to privileges denied to other animals? Were the animals ever completely equal?

116/127	Communication
124/126	Napoleon
124/129	Snowball

126 The whole farm . . .

Given the pigs' known liking for food it is perhaps predictable that their election slogan should concentrate on it. However, notice its sad irony.

122/128	The Rebellion
125/130	Napoleon

Whoever ate well later on, it was certainly not the working animals. Do we have the feeling that Napoleon thought it up on the spur of the moment as a vote-catcher, rather than having any intention of fulfilling his promise? You will recall that much earlier in the story it was Napoleon who very quickly took charge of the distribution of food after the revolution. He obviously sees its control as crucial to his success and power.

127 Apart from the . . .
The debate about defence is one that finds parallels in our own society. Unfortunately, because of the way in which politics at Animal Farm had degenerated into a matter of simply opposing whatever the other party was saying, the animals were unable to make the choice of a sensible balance between both quite valid points of view. It is interesting that Snowball is keen on using propaganda to spread the revolution, but fails to see that Napoleon is using exactly the same technique to undermine his position with the animals. When he is shortly driven from the farm, Napoleon will use those same propaganda techniques to blacken his name and distort the animals' memory of him.

125/136   Communication

128 At last the . . .
This is a key scene. All along, Napoleon had obviously thought that his power was not going to be secure when it was threatened by so eloquent a speaker as Snowball, who could easily move the animals to his way of thinking. The startling shortness of his speech opposing Snowball foreshadows the speed and finality of his real response.

119/129   Meetings
126/129   The Rebellion

129 At last the . . .
Snowball tries to persuade the animals by argument and reason to support building the windmill. He understands its potential and how it would transform the animals' lives. You should compare Snowball's concern for the common good, and his sincerity, with Napoleon's dishonesty and self-interest which reaches its fruition later in the story.

128/130   The Rebellion
124/131   The windmill
125/130   Snowball
128/131   Meetings

130 At last the . . .
Napoleon's quiet confidence suggests his premeditation of the dogs' attack on Snowball which follows. His treachery and cruelty are quite obvious. Even at this stage, could the animals have defended Snowball and changed the course of Napoleon's rise to power?

129/131   The Rebellion
126/133   Napoleon
129/132   Snowball

131 At last the . . .
It is Snowball's passionate appeal for the windmill that triggers Napoleon's signal to the dogs to attack Snowball, underlining the seriousness of the windmill issue. This key scene is something of a watershed. The mood of both the animals' meetings and the whole fable, changes; from now on the atmosphere is one of threat and fear, rather than hope and positive idealism.

130/132   The Rebellion
129/132   Meetings
129/145   The windmill

132 At this there . . .
Snowball's banishment leaves the animals at Napoleon's mercy. It is worth speculating if events might have turned out differently had Snowball been a little less carried away with his plans and more involved in the practicalities of running Animal Farm. Equally, do you feel that Boxer, Benjamin and

131/133   The Rebellion
130/167   Snowball
131/134   Meetings

Clover could have contributed more than selfish cynicism and blind loyalty to the 'state'?

---

133 Silent and terrified, . . .
It is a pity that no one had the presence of mind to ask Napoleon what he was doing with the puppies he had taken into his care! However, note the foreshadowing of Napoleon's change into a 'human' in the way the dogs relate to him just as other dogs had done with Mr Jones.

132/134	The Rebellion
130/139	Napoleon

---

134 Napoleon, with the . . .
The expulsion of Snowball is the beginning of Napoleon's reign of terror and bloodshed. It is at this stage that the pigs separate from the other animals to take over the management of farm affairs. The nature of future meetings is different from now on. How would you describe the purpose of the future Sunday meetings of the animals and how are they basically different from earlier meetings?

133/135	The Rebellion
132/136	Meetings

---

135 Napoleon, with the . . .
The reference to the platform from which Old Major first spoke to the animals should prompt the reader to look at the betrayal of the ideal. Compare the two events and see just how far the revolution has come and how well it has fulfilled Old Major's dream.

134/136	The Rebellion
32/143	Old Major

---

136 Napoleon, with the . . .
What used to be an occasion when the animals would decide the work to be done is suddenly turned on its head. Now the animals come for their orders. The freedom to debate, and therefore to disagree, is immediately abolished, and with it virtually everything the revolution had promised them. Saluting the flag and the singing of their anthem is no longer a pleasure but a duty. You need to compare this situation with the animals' joy in those two things just after the Battle of the Cowshed to gain a measure of how far they have fallen.

127/138	Communication
135/137	The Rebellion
134/137	Meetings

---

137 In spite of . . .
A number of the animals were unhappy at the turn of events but found themselves unable to express their thoughts clearly. Boxer had the same problem. If they had learned their lessons in literacy more effectively, perhaps, even now they could have put up a better opposition to Napoleon's plans. As it is, only the four young porkers begin to protest but, in face of threats from the dogs, they subside. Perhaps they would have been better to make their protest, at least they would have been heard. As it is, Napoleon will ensure that they pay the ultimate price for their opposition to him. Notice what happens to them later. Any chance of rescuing the revolution from Napoleon is destroyed when the sheep set up their mindless bleating and prevent anyone from saying anything of value. Do the animals now have little choice but to submit to Napoleon and his dogs, and do they see the situation in those terms?

136/143	Meetings
136/145	The Rebellion

---

138 In spite of . . .
Consider the importance of the dogs' threatening growls, together with the sheep's noisy bleating, every time there is any sort of protest or challenge to

136/139	Communication
118/233	The sheep

the pigs. Under a dictatorship what sort of threatening person would the dogs represent?

---

139 Afterwards Squealer was . . .
None of the animals dispute that Comrade Napoleon believes all animals are equal. Neither do they object to the idea that whereas they might make mistakes, Napoleon could not. Suddenly, he has become more than just an animal – is this a step towards his being declared a god (or a human)? Squealer will now become very prominent in organizing the new society, a position which ensures that Napoleon will become even more unapproachable and secure in his power.

138/140	Communication
133/143	Napoleon
104/140	Squealer

---

140 'Bravery is not . . .'
The importance of a literate, thoughtful population who actually make use of their brains is soon to be demonstrated. Consider the propagandist skill with which Squealer subtly puts over his lies, half-truths and omissions to keep the animals docile and in agreement with the pigs' plans for them. If they had just been slightly less docile and critical of their own abilities they might have stood a chance against Squealer.

| 139/141 | Communication |
| 139/141 | Squealer |

---

141 'Bravery is not . . .'
The question that Squealer so frequently puts to the animals about whether or not they want Jones back is used to reinforce whatever argument Squealer is trying to put over. It acts as the ultimate threat and increasingly the only point upon which both the pigs and animals agree. Jones, in his absence, becomes the unknown fear that unites, momentarily, all the animals when it is considered necessary to do so. Is it an argument that will eventually lose its force – if the animals ever manage to think about it?

99/185	Mr Jones
140/142	Squealer
140/142	Communication

---

142 Once again this . . .
Already, Boxer and the other animals are beginning to doubt their own memories in favour of Squealer's lies. With a brain unused to thinking, Boxer decides that Napoleon's words must be right. Given the position of respect in which the other animals hold him, Boxer's adoption of the maxim 'Napoleon is always right' is disastrous. Can you see why? The addition of his own private maxim, to work harder, underlines his assumption that hard work will ensure that everything can be solved. Unfortunately, a lack of good sense will ensure that his hard work amounts to very little in terms of furthering the true spirit of the revolution.

107/151	Boxer
141/144	Squealer
141/144	Communication

---

143 By this time . . .
The animals are 'required' to pay homage to the skull of Old Major each Sunday morning. This 'uses' the respect in which Old Major was held to reinforce Napoleon's authority over the animals, specifically for the week's orders. Note the organization of the Sunday meetings and who sits where. There has been a great change in these meetings since the first one so long ago. You might like to consider other places of authority that you know of, Parliament, law courts, council chambers, and comment upon the rituals, seating arrangements and furnishings and their significance in that context.

137/154	Meetings
139/146	Napoleon
135/251	Old Major

---

144 By this time . . .
Note how, protected by the strength of the dogs, Napoleon keeps by him the

| 142/145 | Communication |

other props to his authority: Squealer, with his talent for propaganda and another pig, Minimus, who supposedly had a gift for writing songs and poems. No doubt his talents will soon be put to use.

142/146	Squealer

145 On the third . . .
The announcement that the windmill was to be built after all came as a surprise to the animals, so much so that the announcements accompanying it pass without comment. It is, however, a clear warning to them, if they bothered to listen, that the next two years were going to be hard work, and on a smaller ration of food. Be aware of how frequently Napoleon uses food as a means of control and influence.

144/146	Communication
137/147	The Rebellion
131/151	The windmill

146 That evening Squealer . . .
Napoleon changes his mind about the plans to build the windmill. Whilst Snowball was leading the project, Napoleon opposed it vigorously, but now that Snowball has been expelled from Animal Farm, Napoleon can safely support the project. He obviously recognized its potential value for the farm. The unnecessary distortion of the truth combined with self-praise, albeit actually spoken by Squealer, are the hallmark of every dictator in modern history.

145/147	Communication
143/148	Napoleon
144/156	Squealer

147 That evening Squealer . . .
From now on the dogs repeat their threatening behaviour when required to do so. A combination of the threat of physical violence and political propaganda, largely comprised of half-truths and downright lies, ensures the animals' acceptance of Napoleon's demands. Is the spirit of the Rebellion, 'all animals are equal', completely dead at this stage?

146/148	Communication
145/149	The Rebellion

148 That evening Squealer . . .
Napoleon's 'doubletalk' is calculated to deceive the animals, but it should not deceive the reader. In his portrayal of Napoleon, Orwell comes closest to making us aware of how he feels power-hungry politicians behave.

147/155	Communication
146/154	Napoleon

Chapter 6

149 All that year . . .
What do you think of the animals working like slaves and being happy in their work? This is understandable because they believe they are working for themselves, whereas in reality . . . ? Structurally, at the end of chapter 5, we have a neat division of the story into two halves. In chapter 1 the animals were slaving away for Farmer Jones: they rebelled, improved their lot, saw democracy come, and, by the last chapter, go! Now they reassure themselves that all is well because they are not working for a 'pack of idle, thieving human beings'. This is true, but for whom are they working? From now until the end of the story their lot will become harder and harder whilst the pigs transform themselves – into what?

147/150	The Rebellion

150 Throughout the spring . . .
Note the punishment of the animals by the tampering with their rations; we would surely say that this was a denial of basic rights, but the animals accept it as their lot in life. How much of this acceptance is due to early conditioning? There is an obvious and outrageously unfair contradiction in a ruling that says work is strictly voluntary – but you will be punished if you don't do it; however, with Boxer determined to work harder and Benjamin presumably not prepared to comment, who is there to protest at the ruling?

151 The windmill presented . . .
The building of the windmill involves an enormous effort on the part of the animals, especially Boxer. Given that the animals are virtually forced to labour over it every day of the week, the description here of breaking stones by desperately slow and hard physical labour reminds one of the stone-breaking that convicts have traditionally been forced to do when sentenced to 'hard labour'. Would you agree that whilst the animals do not yet realize it, they are effectively treated as convicts, albeit at the moment with their full cooperation?

152 But it was . . .
Boxer's Herculean efforts to move the boulders uphill begin to tell on his physique. His strength and moral determination help him to succeed but his reliance on maxims for guidance limit his awareness of what is happening to him and to the other animals on the farm. Perhaps this combination of attributes positively aid the process of corruption, especially when that strength and moral determination are totally unsupported by any form of logical thought or basic common sense?

153 But it was . . .
Clover realizes that Boxer is overworking. Throughout, she often has enough understanding of events to make her suffer but not sufficient to alter what happens. She lacks the imagination to see the pigs for what they are. Boxer's pride in his labours leads him to work on the windmill out of working hours. Does he do this because he is intellectually convinced of how valuable the windmill will be, or because hard physical labour somehow makes it unnecessary for him to think and worry about what is happening all around him?

154 One Sunday morning . . .
Napoleon's 'new policy' of trading with neighbouring farms effectively breaks the animals' first Commandment – what is it? That the needs of the windmill must override everything else contains the notion that the end justifies the means. That is, if what you are attempting to achieve can only be accomplished through actions you might rather not take or which are undoubtedly wrong, you ignore those facts and say the result will justify the actions you take. It is, to say the least, a dangerous philosophy, but one that has been, and still is, frequently used to justify all sorts of events taking place. It is typical that Napoleon should be quick to see its value! As before, this latest announcement is used to lessen the impact of another announcement, this time the proposed sale of the hens' eggs.

155 Once again the . . .
Be aware of the growing suppression of all opposition to Napoleon's authority and note the mixture of threats (which are real enough) and reasoning (which appears to be fair but which, in reality, is not) that characterizes Napoleon's dealings with the animals. They do not appear to notice the subtle changes that have altered the whole format of the meetings; have you?

156 Afterwards Squealer made . . .
Instead of discussion, Squealer informs individual animals of decisions taken. How does this reduce opposition or challenge to any decisions or orders made by the pigs? Mass disruption by the sheep combined with the 'warning off' of individuals is a very effective way of silencing opposition. Consider the significance of Squealer persuading the animals to doubt their own memories. Note how he asks them, 'have you any record of such a resolution?'. The question is hugely significant and ironic in view of Snowball's attempt to make the animals literate and their abysmal failure to rise to his vision.

157 Every Monday Mr Whymper . . .
Notice the reaction of the animals to Napoleon giving orders to a man. Does this help to explain some of their acceptance of his position as dictator? Note the pride they took in the fact that 'on all fours' Napoleon gave orders to a human. They will have little time to enjoy the sight!

158 Every Monday Mr Whymper . . .
Mr Whymper's involvement with the farm is crucial to the development of Napoleon's relationships with the surrounding farmers. Slyness and opportunism are Whymper's main qualities. Do you think his name also suggests other aspects of character? Like all the other humans, he is very lightly drawn so as not to overshadow the animals whose story this is.

159 Every Monday Mr Whymper . . .
The windmill inspires jealousy in the humans and later on it is destroyed by Frederick. However, in the meantime, with the other farmers Pilkington and Frederick now begin to accept Animal Farm. What are some possible reasons for this change of loyalties?

160 It was about . . .
The rest of the animals might not have attained Utopia, but with the pigs now having moved into the farmhouse and sleeping in beds, it would appear that *they* have! Note the recurring argument used by Squealer that because the pigs were involved in 'brainwork' they needed special facilities. Can you remember when he last used this argument to justify something the pigs were doing? What do you think of the reason for special privilege? You ought to distinguish between facilities necessary to carry out a particular task of work and those which are concerned with the progression towards a luxurious life-style.

161 It was about . . .
Boxer is content to fall back on his maxim which has elevated Napoleon to a god-like position. Clover, however, still has a few memories of the revolutionary ideals left and tries to check the Commandments. Yet again,

the value of literacy is obvious – she has to get Muriel to read to her. The change to the Commandment puzzles her but, because it is written down, she accepts it. It is perhaps fitting and somewhat ironic that Muriel, whom we met much earlier reading newspaper scraps collected from the garbage heap to the other animals, should find nothing strange about the latest piece of rubbish she reads. Is this the first of the Commandments to have been changed?

153/162	Clover
0/194	Muriel

162 'You have heard . . .'
Was it a coincidence that Squealer should happen to be near Clover when it was necessary to 'put the whole matter in its proper perspective'? Is this a hint of the surveillance we associate with a state run by a dictator?

161/168	Clover
156/163	Squealer

163 'You have heard . . .'
The arguments used by Squealer to convince the other animals do not vary overmuch; he obviously feels no need to change his style of presentation – yet. His justification of sleeping in a bed by defining it merely as a place to sleep, carefully ignores the luxury and unnatural aspect of a human bed as a place for an animal to sleep. Equally obvious to us but not to the animals is the bankrupt distinction he draws between sheets and blankets. The animals find such arguments difficult to refute. It would need someone like Snowball, who was used to using his brain, to see the gaping holes in the reasons that Squealer puts forward for these departures from the spirit of the revolution – hence another good reason for Snowball's expulsion. Note the phrase that clinches the animals' acceptance of Squealer's words – you must have seen it a few times now. Can you remember on which occasions?

161/168	Communication
161/164	The Rebellion
162/171	Squealer

164 By the autumn . . .
The windmill gives a great sense of purpose and achievement to the animals. Apart from its mechanical benefits, it might also give them a feeling of equality with human society. Also consider the importance of the windmill to Napoleon's ego and status in relation to the other farmers. Equally, the neighbouring farmers and their animals will also have different reactions – can you think what they will be?

163/170	The Rebellion
159/165	The windmill

165 By the autumn . . .
One begins to wonder at the state of Boxer's mind. Can his action of working in moonlight be justified in any way at all? Note the huge contrast between his attitude and Benjamin's. Why is Benjamin so unenthusiastic about the windmill? He comes closest of all the animals to seeing the events in the story from the reader's point of view, but just how much foresight can we reasonably claim for him? In some senses is he about as useful as Mollie but more dangerous to the Rebellion? At least everyone can see Mollie for what she is, whereas the cynicism and total lack of positive thought or action on Benjamin's part towards the aim of the Rebellion could well have a negative effect on the other animals.

164/166	The windmill
102/186	Benjamin
161/168	Boxer

166 With one accord . . .
For all sorts of reasons the ruin of the windmill is disastrous for the animals – but, was Napoleon involved in its destruction? He was first on the scene, racing everyone to the site of the disaster, a most unusual action. He is quick to blame Snowball, who provides him with a useful scapegoat for all sorts of occasions in the future. Pig footprints were discovered close by

165/167	The windmill
157/167	Napoleon

leading to a hole in the hedge. If Snowball hadn't destroyed the windmill to whom did the footprints belong? All is most definitely not clear!

167 'Comrades,' he said . . .
Like many dictators, Napoleon has an inability to admit any mistakes or error of judgment. In Snowball, he now has someone who can be blamed for whatever goes wrong or whatever mistakes are made by Napoleon. Snowball can be used as an awful example to the animals and the witch-hunt for him can deflect the animals' attention from other matters.

166/201	The windmill
166/169	Napoleon
132/176	Snowball

Chapter 7

168 Out of spite, . . .
Boxer and Clover are in something of a fool's paradise. Both sides of the new animal society find inspiration in Boxer's strength; the pigs for purposes of exploitation and propaganda, the other animals for reassurance and a heartening example. Is this really what Old Major dreamed of for his new society? Note the tired old clichés that Squealer trots out – 'the joy of service and the dignity of labour'. Whenever somebody who is not personally involved in a particular task describes it as a joy, as dignified, as a service to the community or any one of a hundred similar clichés, then you can probably assume that those carrying out the task are being abused in some way, especially if it is so described at the same time as wages and conditions of work are being discussed.

163/170	Communication
165/179	Boxer
162/189	Clover

169 It was vitally . . .
Suddenly, the simple 'virtues' framed in the Seven Commandments take second place to the need to survive. Notice how important Napoleon's dishonesty is in deceiving Whymper so that public confidence in Animal Farm is maintained. Might this be necessary to the survival of Animal Farm?

167/171	Napoleon
158/205	Mr Whymper

170 It was vitally . . .
Who exactly does the deception of Whymper benefit? If the humans had discovered the animals' plight and as a result had successfully invaded Animal Farm would the majority of animals have been worse off? Certainly Napoleon's future would have been bleak but no doubt the rest of the animals would have survived. Ironically, the animals' sacrifices in supporting Napoleon's deception merely help to keep him in power and lead to even greater excesses in the destruction of the revolution's ideals.

168/171	Communication
164/173	The Rebellion

171 Nevertheless, towards the . . .
Napoleon is becoming increasingly remote from the other animals. His infrequent appearances at the Sunday meetings and the ceremonial nature of the few times he does appear help to distance him from the days when he was just one of the animals. The power with which he has surrounded himself, and the power that many dictators wield, is very similar to that exercised by ancient kings and queens who ruled by 'divine right'. That is, they believed their power was given to them by God and they were only answerable to God for their actions. Whatever they decided *had* to be done.

170/177	Communication
169/173	Napoleon
163/172	Squealer
155/182	Meetings

172 Nevertheless, towards the . . .
More than ever Squealer is the only contact the animals have with the élitist pigs. Napoleon is distanced from the day-to-day running of the farm. Squealer, the 'propaganda machine', is the only source of contact between the animals and their ruler. Do you think they now realize that they have a 'ruler'?

171/179   Squealer

173 When the hens . . .
The hens' revolt was doomed to failure from the start. Note how it passes unremarked by Boxer, Clover, Benjamin or any other animal; each is probably too bound up in their own affairs to worry about the hens. Boxer's single-minded fixation with using his strength for but one purpose is a good example of this. No longer are they looking 'outward' to the needs of all their fellow animals, but 'inward' to what they consider important for themselves. Napoleon's demand that the hens sacrifice their eggs and the success of that demand is a major upset for the revolution's high ideals.

170/174   The Rebellion
171/174   Napoleon

174 When the hens . . .
The idea of trading presupposes a surplus to be traded with, which cuts across Old Major's teaching. Is this just Napoleon facing the realities of the farm's needs? If so how should the reader view the sale of eggs? Perhaps the author is pointing out the genuine difficulties of putting ideals into practice?

173/178   The Rebellion
173/175   Napoleon

175 All this while . . .
What reasons could Napoleon have for his lack of decision over selling timber to either Pilkington or Frederick? He is aware that to do business with one of them will make trading with the other almost impossible and, as yet, he is unable to make up his mind as to which will be the most useful to him in the long term.

174/176   Napoleon
159/199   Pilkington and Frederick

176 All this while . . .
Napoleon steps up the witch-hunt for Snowball, using him as a reason for his own indecisiveness in settling to whom he is going to sell the timber.

175/177   Napoleon
167/177   Snowball

177 Suddenly, early in . . .
The animals are persuaded that Snowball is responsible for all the little mishaps and annoying events that occur at the farm. As a result, Napoleon declares that a full investigation must be set up, thus opening the way for a purge of any animal suspected of being a threat to his rule and making possible an even greater departure from the revolutionary ideals of Old Major.

171/178   Communication
176/181   Napoleon
176/200   Snowball

178 The animals were . . .
The implied threat to the animals' internal security is an essential starting-point for the brutal purge that is about to come. As with any state of the type Animal Farm has become, the rulers remain in power through a whole range of measures. Not least are the twin threats of invasion from enemies outside the country's borders and counter-revolution from enemies of the people within the borders.

177/179   Communication
174/182   The Rebellion

179 'I do not believe . . .'
At last Boxer is stirred to question Squealer's reinterpretation of past events, and Snowball's part in them. Bluntly, he challenges Squealer and refuses to back down when his strong loyalties are threatened. However, note the result of Squealer quoting Comrade Napoleon as confirming the story. Boxer immediately accepts the new version of events. The elevation of Napoleon to a position far above that of an ordinary animal serves its purpose yet again. Boxer's disagreement has been noted by Squealer who now sees him as a potential threat to the security of the pigs' power.

178/180	Communication
168/183	Boxer
172/180	Squealer

180 'That was part . . .'
The importance of appealing to historical evidence, both written and remembered, is an essential part of Squealer's armoury. The only thing the animals now possess is the memory of Old Major's ideals, their memories of events since his death, and the Seven Commandments. It is ironic that Squealer should offer written evidence to support his condemnation of Snowball. He knows that with the animals to whom it did not matter that they could not read, he was safe to offer such worthless evidence. His words 'if you were able to read' highlight both the tragic lack of long-term success for Snowball's literacy drive and Squealer's callous manipulation of that failure. In appealing to the animals' memory, Squealer conveniently forgets the time when he condemned their memory of events and asked them if they had written evidence to support their recollections – can you recall those circumstances?

179/184	Communication
179/191	Squealer

181 Four days later . . .
Napoleon uses medals to enhance his public image – like so many be-medalled and beribboned dictators. None of the medals represent any real bravery or achievement on Napoleon's part, but they do have the cosmetic effect of raising him above any glories that Snowball may have attained and which might still be remembered by the animals.

177/182	Napoleon

182 Napoleon stood sternly . . .
The appalling blood-bath starts, and turns upside down all the hopes expressed for the future by Old Major. The animals are infinitely worse off now than ever they were under Jones's rule. Can you explain in what ways this is so? It is perhaps to be expected that the time for settling debts has arrived! The first assault against members of the 'privileged class', the pigs, is on the one hand vengeance for their outspokenness at an earlier meeting (can you remember which and when?) for these were surely the same four pigs. On the other hand it half prepares the animals for greater excesses, notably an attack on Boxer.

178/184	The Rebellion
181/183	Napoleon
171/183	Meetings

183 Napoleon stood sternly . . .
The attack of the dogs on Boxer comes very shortly after his defence of Snowball. There are some interesting points to note here. It is a measure of how far Boxer's intelligence has been diluted that he is unable to realize that Napoleon planned this attack on him. Amazingly, Boxer looks to Napoleon to see what action should be taken, and on his command lets the dog go. Is there a change here also in the use to which Boxer is prepared to put his strength? Recall how at the Battle of the Cowshed, Boxer was most concerned that he might have killed the stable-boy. Here, he looks to Napoleon to see if he 'should crush the dog to death'. Is all the work that

182/231	Meetings
179/187	Boxer
182/185	Napoleon

Boxer willingly undertakes dulling his awareness of what is happening and turning him into a mere brute?

---

184 The three hens . . .
After the terrible and public execution of the pigs, the animals are affected by a wave of hysteria which leads them to admit crimes that were largely nonsensical. Yet research into similar show trials in modern dictatorships provides evidence of similar public confessions, especially by those who have nothing to gain from them. The confessions have nothing to do with what is right or just, but a great deal to do with injustice and irrational, hysterical fear. Animal Farm has come a long way under Napoleon's leadership!

180/191	Communication
182/187	The Rebellion

---

185 When it was . . .
The animals, even in their shocked state, compare the recent slaughter which was the result of Napoleon's lust for absolute power, with the slaughter for gain in Jones's day. The simple-minded animals recognize the greater horror that has befallen them. How would you define the difference?

141/227	Mr Jones
183/196	Napoleon

---

186 When it was . . .
Benjamin seems to be as shocked and grieved as the other animals at the executions, for all his low opinion of the revolution and the animals' hopes of a new society. It is puzzling to know why he never spoke up before, or even at this moment, while the animals had the potential to cope with the pigs. Could he have taken up the leadership when Snowball was expelled? Would Boxer and Clover have supported him? Or was he a victim of his own self-fulfilling prophecy? There is no way more certain to induce failure than when you say a thing cannot be done and then make no attempt to do it.

165/193	Benjamin

---

187 'I do not . . .'
Boxer, shocked by the confessions and executions, is not frightened by them as are the other animals. However, he misses the significance of what has happened and once more falls back on his selfless resolution to work harder, putting his moral resolve into physical action and thus unwittingly promoting the interests of the corrupt pigs. We have described his actions as selfless; could they also be described as selfish? Has he reached a point where he does not dare try to think about what is happening all around him? If so, is this because he might feel that he was partly to blame?

184/189	The Rebellion
183/204	Boxer

---

188 The animals huddled . . .
Consider the significance of the animals' return to the knoll looking for comfort and reassurance, partly from Clover and partly, perhaps, to confirm in their minds that their original point of view was right. It is interesting to note that Boxer does not join them. As suggested in the previous comment, perhaps he no longer feels part of their ideal? Compare their mood of misery and shock with that of the optimism they expressed so energetically when they previously gathered at this spot.

121/0	The knoll

---

189 The animals huddled . . .
After the slaughter carried out during the purge, the animals turn to Clover. Her thoughts and memories act as a check on the changes that took place in

187/192	The Rebellion
168/190	Clover

the course of the history of Animal Farm. Can you identify the occasions she thinks about and the reasons which led to the failure of the revolution's high ideals?

---

190 The animals huddled . . .
What is the importance of Clover being unable to express her thoughts? If she had succeeded might she have roused the other animals to a final, spirited defence of Old Major's vision?

| 189/193 | Clover |

---

191 They had just . . .
Squealer makes light work of what might have been the difficult task of banning 'Beasts of England'. Revolutionary songs have long been a force which kept alive the flickering hopes of revolutionaries across the world. In abolishing the anthem, Napoleon demonstrates his awareness of its potential danger. Minimus the poet, whose very name suggests that he has minimal talent, provides them with something else to sing; it is far inferior but safe as far as Napoleon is concerned. The new song also illustrates the lack of artistic creativity which is a frequent mark of rule by dictator, and especially so in his early years when the dictator is still not absolutely sure of his firm grasp on the reins of power.

| 184/192 | Communication |
| 180/195 | Squealer |

Chapter 8

192 A few days . . .
How many of the Commandments and Old Major's ideals have now been broken? The sixth Commandment is a crucial one, and once broken the last one will not stand for much longer. Resolutions about life being precious and sacred are typical of revolutionaries, and of religions, societies, governments and nations of all colour and creed. Yet how many of them have sooner or later made exceptions to this fundamental rule when they felt it convenient?

| 191/193 | Communication |
| 189/194 | The Rebellion |

---

193 A few days . . .
Why should Benjamin refuse to 'meddle' when Clover asks him to read the sixth Commandment? It was hardly a crime, yet, to read them. It is however, a measure of the depths to which the animals have descended that they are now frightened to read.

192/194	Communication
186/211	Benjamin
190/194	Clover

---

194 A few days . . .
Muriel again helps Clover by reading the sixth Commandment to her. When did she previously do this? As always, Clover can remember better than the others, but not quite well enough. The lack of ability to read and write have ensured that there is only one copy of the Commandments and thus no written check on what they originally said. The tremendous importance of Snowball's priority in trying to make the animals literate can now be fully

193/195	Communication
192/196	The Rebellion
193/225	Clover
161/222	Muriel

appreciated. Its lesson for our own society is not something that should be overlooked. What sort of dangers would you say might result from living in a society where there is a huge gulf between those who have wealth, power and education, and those who have not?

195 Throughout that year . . .

Do we believe Squealer's 'lists of figures' read from some paper? He can say whatever it suits the pigs to say. Who is there to contradict him now?

194/197	Communication
191/200	Squealer

196 All orders were . . .

Note Napoleon's withdrawal from the other animals, even the pigs, and the image he projects when he does appear. To all he becomes something larger than life. He has used Animalism and the revolution to feed his ego and to institute a régime which serves his every wish. His authority is now absolute.

194/198	The Rebellion
185/197	Napoleon

197 Napoleon was now . . .

Though the flattering names given to Napoleon may sound ridiculous to us, they are well within the experience of 20th-century society! The fawning poem, 'Comrade Napoleon' is of poor literary quality, cliché-ridden and full of meaningless nationalism and phrasing which tries to imitate good poetry. If it wasn't so vain and serious it would be funny. Unfortunately, the animals are unable to appreciate how easily it could have been used to undermine the leader's authority and dignity.

195/198	Communication
196/202	Napoleon

198 Meanwhile, through the . . .

Can you think of anything more unlikely than that three small hens should realistically plot to kill a pig of Napoleon's size? Effectively, it is merely a ritual slaughter that the pigs are indulging in. Its purpose is to demonstrate and confirm them in their power, and to keep the other animals in fear and terror. It acts as a deterrent to any animal who might be contemplating revolution, but does not excite any awkward enquiries such as the death of Boxer, Clover or another important animal might. The death of a few hens, when there are so many, will not have any adverse affect on the egg production. It is typical of such a society that the weakest are the most oppressed.

197/200	Communication
196/201	The Rebellion

199 At about the same time . . . .

Napoleon's apparent decision to sell the timber to Pilkington is accompanied by a series of rumours about the cruel nature of Frederick and the way he mistreats his animals. Note that the rumours are similar to those which were spread about Animal Farm in its early days. The details sound more as if they came from Squealer's propaganda machine rather than bearing any relationship to the truth of the matter. Would you agree that the rumours are put about merely to justify Napoleon's dealings with Pilkington rather than Frederick? Be aware that until later in the book we do not actually meet Pilkington or Frederick. Most of what we know of them is hearsay.

175/202	Pilkington and Frederick

200 Nevertheless, feeling against . . .

Do be aware of the deeply sinister side of Squealer's part in the post-revolution society – pointed to here by the suicide of the gander. The number of political activists throughout the world who manage to commit 'suicide'

198/214	Communication
177/202	Snowball
195/214	Squealer

whilst in the custody of oppressive régimes is quite remarkable. Note how none of the activities going on around the animals is at all creative. Apart from their work the only other events are the continuing blackening of Snowball's character, death-threat slogans directed against Frederick and news of plots and suicide. Compare this to the hive of creative activity which Snowball encouraged. The animals' social and cultural environment is a very dreary one indeed.

201 In the autumn, . . .

The completion of the mill is a great triumph for the animals and for Napoleon, but can you see how it presents something of a problem to him? Until now, he was able to keep the animals occupied with this tremendous endeavour which pushed all other thoughts, ambitions and ideals into the background. Now it is finished, will the animals have leisure to start contemplating where the Rebellion has got them and whether their lives have improved since the expulsion of Jones? Napoleon identifies himself with the success by a ceremonial appearance and naming it Napoleon Mill. Note however the prophetic irony of the remark – 'Nothing short of explosives . . .'.

198/202	The Rebellion
167/210	The windmill

202 All relations with . . .

In considering Napoleon's double-dealing with Pilkington and Frederick be aware of how one act of treachery leads to another. Note also the convenience of having the absent Snowball as a repository for discarded ideas when 'adjustments' to the truth have to be made. Snowball may have been a threat to Napoleon when he was at Animal Farm but now that he has gone, he is proving to be an asset to Napoleon's and Squealer's propaganda.

201/204	The Rebellion
197/203	Napoleon
200/234	Snowball
199/203	Pilkington and Frederick

203 Meanwhile the timber . . .

The almost undue speed with which the timber is removed from Animal Farm ought to suggest to the reader that all is not well. Napoleon seems to have met his match with Frederick who is as amoral as Napoleon. It is perhaps not unreasonable to suggest that Napoleon made the mistake of thinking he was dealing with illiterate, bemused animals and not with fellow 'dictators'.

202/207	Napoleon
202/206	Pilkington and Frederick

204 Meanwhile the timber . . .

Note how the authenticity of the bank-notes seems to be indirectly queried by Boxer.

202/217	The Rebellion
187/209	Boxer

205 Three days later . . .

Whymper, as well as Napoleon, is deceived over the timber sale. Does this suggest that he is not accepted amongst the other humans? This could throw some light on his character and explain how he might have initially come to volunteer his services to Napoleon.

169/0	Mr Whymper

206 The very next morning . . .

Consider the importance of Frederick's cowardly attack on Animal Farm. Supposing he had won the battle of the windmill, what different endings can you imagine to the fable? Having been the subject of a bitter character assassination at Animal Farm before the timber deal was signed and not trusted to pay by cheque, Frederick then pays by forged notes which no one thinks to check, and follows up with a successful attack on the windmill, if

111/208	Conflicts
203/210	Pilkington and Frederick

not Animal Farm. Despite the ferocity of the battle, could there have been any scheming by Napoleon and Frederick? Remember the comment we made about the windmill being perhaps an embarrassment to Napoleon.

---

207 Napoleon called the . . .
In an endeavour to retain his prestige amongst the animals Napoleon announces the death penalty on Frederick. How serious do you think this threat is? The placing of the sentries and the message to Pilkington increase the animals' awareness of the need to prepare for war.

203/209	Napoleon

---

208 The very next . . .
The Battle of the Windmill is an all-out attack by the humans, especially when compared with previous battles. The superior weapons of the humans are easily able to drive back the animals and for once Napoleon seems unable to cope.

206/209	Conflicts

---

209 The very next . . .
This time Boxer and Napoleon are linked together in the defence of the farm as Boxer and Snowball were for the Battle of the Cowshed. Boxer never recognizes his own value or potential for doing good. This lack of self-awareness and undervaluing of himself is Boxer's greatest fault.

208/213	Conflicts
204/214	Boxer
207/210	Napoleon

---

210 Meanwhile Frederick and . . .
The destruction of the windmill by Frederick serves to confirm at least some of Napoleon's propaganda to the working animals about the threat to them from humans, and does help us to understand some of their acceptance of Napoleon's domination.

201/211	The windmill
209/212	Napoleon
206/259	Pilkington and Frederick

---

211 But Benjamin was . . .
Is there an air of self-satisfaction in Benjamin's apparent 'amusement' at the anticipated destruction of the windmill? Certainly, it serves to confirm his negative outlook on the animals' attempt to set up their own farm.

210/249	The windmill
193/223	Benjamin

---

212 Terrified, the animals . . .
Why do you think that Napoleon was the only animal who did not cower from the explosion and hide his face? Is it possible that he knew what was coming, or perhaps that he had suddenly become a very brave dictator?

210/213	Napoleon

---

213 At this sight . . .
The destruction of the windmill enrages the animals and unites them for one last effort to defeat the invading force. You should check back to the previous invasions of Animal Farm and compare the animals' motives on those occasions with their rage and cry for vengeance this time. The mood of the battle is also quite different with its 'savage, bitter' fighting which results in a high casualty rate. Despite his 'courage' when the windmill was blown up, Napoleon is back in his accustomed place directing operations from the rear. Compare his tail 'chipped by a pellet' here, with Snowball's blood-dripping wounds at the Battle of the Cowshed. Napoleon is a complex character and many of his actions are rarely quite what they seem to be.

209/214	Conflicts
212/216	Napoleon

214 As they approached . . .
Not for the first time, Squealer's actions conflict with his words. Conspicuous by his absence in the Battle of the Windmill he has the gall to claim it as a victory for the long-suffering animals. However, as Boxer's memory of the battle is so fresh and crystal clear, this time he challenges Squealer's view and does not seem to have the same problem in getting his brain to work. Perhaps if he had been moved to anger earlier in the story he might have been able to use this brain rather than deciding that 'brainwork' was something beyond him. Do you think the animals have won back what they had before? For the first time we see Boxer actually thinking about the implications of past events and coming to the realization that he was getting older – and perhaps wiser?

215 'What victory, comrade?'
Notice the ambiguity of Squealer's speech; 'victory' is one of those words that are open to several interpretations. What he says is correct, but is it right? Who has gained? Who has lost? The meanings of words like justice, terrorist, freedom fighter, freedom, often depend on someone's individual point of view or position in a particular society. How would you rate the victory at the Battle of the Windmill?

216 But when the . . .
Notice how the unification of the animals is engineered; symbols of victory and patriotism are used to manipulate the animals' feelings. Napoleon becomes such a symbol and he also creates another, the 'Order of the Green Banner'.

217 It was a few . . .
The post-battle propaganda by Napoleon and the whisky celebration by the pigs, which excludes the working animals, are examples of the division between leaders and led. Alcohol has been the cause of suffering in the past. It is not shared with the other animals. Is there a suggestion here that part of the victory has been the pigs over the animals?

218 It was a few . . .
Are Napoleon's drunken aspirations suggested by his wearing of Jones's bowler hat? Typical of the now completely corrupt leadership is Napoleon's illness; it is obviously an almighty hangover and the resultant decree that drinking alcohol was punishable by death is equally as swiftly reversed with the announcement that Napoleon has ordered brewing equipment. It is quite obvious that Animal Farm is now being run for the convenience of the pigs – and Napoleon in particular. Even Napoleon's drunkenness is blamed on Snowball.

219 By the evening, . . .
The full extent of the pigs' contempt for the animals' welfare is revealed when Napoleon uses the intended retirement grazing ground as a field for barley from which whisky can be made. Compared with the animals' conditions at this time it is a particularly ironic example of the sort of discrepancy between what is considered to be essential for rulers and those they rule.

220 By the evening, . . .

One of the main causes of Jones's poor management of the farm and consequent neglect of the animals was his drinking. Here the link between life before and after the revolution is made. Whereas Jones's drinking caused the exploitation and hardship of the animals due to his careless neglect, now Napoleon and the pigs' drinking causes the exploitation and hardship of the animals due to Napoleon's calculated greed. Why should this be far more ominous for the animals' welfare than anything that Jones had in mind?

219/223 The Rebellion

221 About this time . . .

When Squealer held the paint pot for Snowball and stood behind him on the ladder he was slightly more successful than he is now. How many of the Commandments have now been altered and can you remember the occasions when the alterations were discovered? Look at the very detailed description in the story of what the animals saw when they came out to investigate the cause of the loud crash. Yet none of them 'could form any idea' as to the cause of the crash! With the evidence of Squealer's activities so blatantly displayed before them, their reaction is almost unbelievable. Certainly, if nothing else, it marks the degree to which they are now unable to think for themselves. Only Benjamin still has the presence of mind to recognize what is happening.

219/222 Communication
215/238 Squealer

222 But a few days . . .

Muriel's total acceptance of the fifth Commandment highlights the casual way in which the animals now disregard their own memories in favour of Squealer's inventions.

221/226 Communication
194/0 Muriel

Chapter 9

223 Boxer's split hoof . . .

Despite their callous treatment by the pigs, the animals still have a real concern for each other. For once, Benjamin openly expresses concern, but really about a very minor thing. Is Boxer's hoof so much more worthy of his comment than the manipulation of the revolution and the oppression of the farm animals?

220/226 The Rebellion
211/238 Benjamin
214/224 Boxer

224 Boxer's split hoof . . .

Boxer's selflessness and workmanlike pride once more come in to play, much to the concern of his lifelong companions, Clover and Benjamin. Yet again, he dreams of the completion of the windmill and the fulfilment of a promised retirement. Why can he not see, after years of frustrated promises, the absolute impossibility of attaining such objectives if he leaves the matter within the pigs' control?

223/232 Boxer

225 Boxer's split hoof . . .
Clover realizes what Boxer needs but is unable to help him enough. She is concerned in a straightforward and practical way. Compare her sympathy and 'poultice of herbs' with the pigs' indifference and 'pink medicine' later on.

| 194/232 | Clover |

226 Meanwhile life was . . .
Note the implications of the inequality of the food rations and the cunning but false justification for it. How often in history and today do we read of just such a situation? One does not have to look far from home, and to governments of all political persuasions, to recognize the shrill assurances and lists of figures which 'prove' that the standard of living, health care, education etc, have improved almost beyond recognition – in the face of day-to-day experience that things have, if anything, actually got worse. Yet the animals believe every word of it – they are not unlike their modern, human counterparts.

| 222/227 | Communication |
| 223/228 | The Rebellion |

227 Meanwhile life was . . .
The threat of Jones still works with the animals, as does the comparison between post-revolution life and the bad old days under Jones, to underline the pigs' success, and to underpin their power. By now the animals are too confused to trust even their own memories as they have been submitted to so much propaganda and distortion of the truth.

| 226/231 | Communication |
| 185/229 | Mr Jones |

228 There were many . . .
The young pigs are distanced from all other animals and are to be the new élite, but what are the disadvantages to the pigs themselves of such isolation? Note how the privileges and status which is given to the pigs is creating a 'superior' class of animals better catered for than the other animals in every aspect of their lives.

| 226/229 | The Rebellion |

229 The farm had . . .
By now, Napoleon's standard of living far exceeds anything Jones ever dreamed of. Looking back to chapter 1 we see that Old Major was right, the animals *could* manage the farm better than man, but he did not allow for the worst side of the pigs' character coming so strongly into play. Nor did he allow for the fact of differing ambitions and abilities on the part of the animals.

228/230	The Rebellion
227/230	Mr Jones
219/234	Napoleon

230 The farm had . . .
Notice how wistfully the animals still hope for better things from the pigs here. Notice too how callously indifferent the pigs are to the needs and the feelings of the working animals. Compare this with the instance of Jones's careless benevolence in putting surplus milk in the hens' mash. Jones demonstrated the evils of drink, but the pigs seemed not to have learned the lesson.

| 229/235 | The Rebellion |
| 229/0 | Mr Jones |

231 But if there . . .
'Spontaneous Demonstration' is an ironic comment on the freedoms which the animals have lost. What do you think was actually demonstrated, and to whom? Do songs, speeches and processions make life 'dignified' or do they

| 227/232 | Communication |
| 183/233 | Meetings |

merely give the animals something meaningless to do, keeping them and their minds occupied so they will not think of their empty bellies?

232 But if there . . .
What is the importance of Clover and Boxer's part in the 'Spontaneous Demonstration'? What idea would it convey to the animals?

231/234	Communication
224/237	Boxer
225/237	Clover

233 But if there . . .
Despite the demonstrations being supposedly 'spontaneous', the behaviour of the sheep is the same as ever!

| 231/247 | Meetings |
| 138/252 | The sheep |

234 In April, Animal . . .
The declaration of a Republic and the 'election' of Napoleon to President was a fairly predictable result of his insatiable desire for power and glory. That same desire for glory leads to the final mockery of all that Snowball represented when it is announced that he actually led Farmer Jones's men in the assault on Animal Farm. It also shows the pigs' utter contempt for the other animals and the degree to which they feel so totally secure in their position of power.

232/236	Communication
229/239	Napoleon
202/0	Snowball

235 In the middle . . .
Moses' return to Animal Farm and the reintroduction of the delights of Sugarcandy Mountain need some explanation. As has been mentioned before, to some extent Moses represents what the author feels to be the more corrupt aspects of organized religion. However, why should the pigs almost welcome his return and his unsettling effect on the animals? First, note the similarities between Jones's attitude and that of the pigs; effectively they both treat him as a pet with an association and identification of religion with the upper or ruling classes. Also, the pigs are quite happy if the animals are concerned with striving for a better afterlife if it does not affect their work here, and they possibly quite welcome the distraction that Moses provides from the animals' empty stomachs. Is the author making a satirical reference to the use of bread and wine in Christian religious practice when he mentions that Jones fed Moses on crusts soaked in beer, and the pigs fed him on beer?

| 230/247 | The Rebellion |
| 47/0 | Moses |

236 After his hoof . . .
The gradual weakening of Boxer comes at a time when the pigs' power is virtually unquestioned and the revolutionary ideals, for the majority of the animals, have been extinguished. All that Boxer can look forward to is his retirement. Ironically, it is the one thing the pigs will allow him, but not quite in the way he expected.

| 234/239 | Communication |

237 About half the . . .
Clover recognizes the seriousness of Boxer's condition but not the hopelessness of expecting the pigs to give any substantial help or sympathy. It is evident that neither of them has learned much from their experiences over the past years.

| 232/238 | Boxer |
| 232/241 | Clover |

238 All the other . . .
Squealer's response to Boxer's illness gives the animals a moment of concern. However, the very experienced Squealer has no difficulty in persuading them that their worries are groundless. Benjamin demonstrates his love and concern for Boxer by staying with him and keeping the flies away. No doubt he felt he was being very helpful. Would he have been of more help if he had used his brains to try and warn the animals, particularly Boxer, of what the pigs were doing to Old Major's ideals?

239 For the next . . .
Napoleon shows his callousness and indifference to suffering in his premeditated disposal of Boxer. Even for the sake of a public relations exercise he cannot bring himself to visit Boxer; he merely arranges a bottle of pink medicine from Jones's medicine chest to be sent over: medicine that was about as useful to Boxer as the green ribbons the pigs wore on their tails every Sunday.

240 'Fools! Fools!' shouted . . .
Spurred into positive action by the danger to his friend, Boxer, Benjamin reveals the truth of Boxer's removal. Benjamin's role is not always clear. Could he not have convinced Boxer to use his strength against the pigs for the animals' good? What held him back from using his intelligence and the knowledge it gave him of what was really happening at Animal Farm?

241 That gave the . . .
Too late, Benjamin for once pushes Muriel aside and reads the clearly-written message out to the assembled animals. For so long inactive, when he does stir himself to action it is too late, and he does too little. It is Clover who races after the van and calls on Boxer to try to escape – but in vain. And what happens after this? Nothing. There is no attempt to rouse the animals against the pigs, no protest, nothing. Benjamin gives up, as do the other animals. Is there any hope for their future? Do they deserve hope? Be careful how you answer the latter question. It is easy to criticize, but not as easy to become a martyr to a cause.

242 A cry of horror . . .
Can you remember the first appearance of Boxer? Look back and see what remark the author made about Boxer in the same sentence that he mentioned the white stripe on his face. Was it a warning to the reader of what to expect from Boxer, or is it perhaps rather a harsh judgment on an animal that did its best?

243 All the animals . . .
Horribly reminiscent of the mobile extermination vans used by Hitler in the 1930s for his 'final solution', the knacker's van starts to take Boxer away. At last he seems to realize the truth of what is in store for him but too late.

244 All the animals . . .
Ironically those who could help Boxer choose not to. The horses pulling the van behave as Boxer always has, by disregarding everything except their allotted task, and with comparable results.

245 'It was the . . .'
Squealer is here at his hypocritical, callous and skilful worst. But he does not take too much time in disposing of Boxer's memory; Napoleon's name is thrust before the animals and Boxer's death becomes a hymn of praise for Napoleon.

238/250   Squealer

246 Napoleon himself appeared . . .
Napoleon associates himself with the grief felt by the animals at Boxer's death and expediently points out Boxer's two maxims. As always he can turn any occasion to his own advantage.

244/250   Communication
239/253   Napoleon
244/0   Boxer

247 On the day . . .
Note the hypocrisy of the memorial banquet being used by the pigs as an excuse to get drunk, whilst the animals get hungrier. A measure of the depths to which the pigs have sunk is the fact that they have taken to drinking whisky. Did Jones ever get drunk on whisky, so far as we know?

233/258   Meetings
235/248   The Rebellion

Chapter 10

248 Years passed. The . . .
In the next two paragraphs we see just how far the Rebellion has failed to achieve its objectives. Note who has survived. Of Benjamin, Clover, Moses, Napoleon and Squealer, only one did not have what seems, in retrospect, to be a cynical disregard for anything except the preservation of their own lives. Is this too harsh a judgment? How would you explain Clover's survival?

247/251   The Rebellion

249 The farm was . . .
Belatedly, the windmill has been completed. Look back to Snowball's vision of its use to benefit the animals and compare the actual use to which it is put. What good has it done the animals who laboured so long to build it? What good is it doing the working animals now? Who does benefit from its creation of energy?

211/0   The windmill

250 Somehow it seemed . . .
Squealer is revealed by the author to be the worst kind of officious bureaucrat, protected by jargon and the inability of most of us to understand the official mind, or to deal with the paperwork produced by it.

246/251   Communication
245/0   Squealer

Characters and ideas previous/next comment

251 As for the . . .
Old Major's vision is still held by the animals, a poignant reminder of the gap between the ideal and the reality. However 'Beasts of England' is once more sung, though in secret, perhaps giving a hint of the revolution going full circle?

250/252	Communication
248/254	The Rebellion
143/260	Old Major

252 One day in . . .
The removal of the sheep to learn a new song should remind us of the time when Napoleon removed the puppies to 'educate' them, and warn us that a major event is about to occur.

251/254	Communication
233/254	The sheep

253 Yes, it was . . .
Do you think the terrified neighing of Clover suggests that at long last she has awoken to what has been happening around her? Or is it that she now cannot distinguish between pig and man? Is there any difference between pig and man? The appearance of Napoleon, walking on just two legs and carrying a whip in his trotter, presents to the animals clearly and without any attempt at deception the position that their leader desires and holds.

241/261	Clover
246/254	Napoleon

254 There was a . . .
Napoleon has achieved what he envied in man – being upright. The moment for protest was, however, lost when the sheep went into their carefully rehearsed routine and chanted continuously until the prospect of protest was lost forever. Be aware of the very important part played by the sheep in the story. Traditionally viewed as stupid and easily led, these very qualities were used by the pigs to turn the sheep into a very efficient tool of the government.

252/255	Communication
253/257	Napoleon
251/256	The Rebellion
252/0	The sheep

255 For once Benjamin . . .
It is ironic that the last time Benjamin is persuaded to read aloud, he reads the death knell for the animals' revolutionary ideals. He, of all animals, is most likely to understand the full implications of it, yet there is no comment. Is one needed?

254/256	Communication
241/0	Benjamin

256 For once Benjamin . . .
The replacement of the Seven Commandments by the now all-important statement of political doctrine, says it all. Can you trace the steps by which the pigs have moved towards this travesty of Old Major's original ideals?

255/260	Communication
254/257	The Rebellion

257 After that it . . .
Consider the importance of Napoleon wearing Jones's clothes, taking on his mantle, as it were. The wearing of Jones's clothing by Napoleon a week before the meeting with the humans, foreshadows that final scene when he will seem to have assumed all Jones's worst characteristics, and be indistinguishable from his arrogant, human guests.

256/258	The Rebellion
254/260	Napoleon

258 That evening loud . . .
The animals and humans meet on terms of equality, but true to the new Commandment not all animals are equal.

257/259	The Rebellion
247/0	Meetings

Characters and ideas previous/next comment

259 It was a source . . .

There is a certain irony in Pilkington congratulating the pigs, not on the efficiency of the farm but on the fact that the animals on Animal Farm did more work on less food than the animals on any other farm. Despite Pilkington's honeyed words, note who falls out with each other at the end of this scene!

260 He did not . . .

Napoleon, having agreed with Pilkington's praise of the wretched conditions endured by the animals, puts the final nails in the coffin of the animals' revolutionary ideals: addressing each other as 'Comrade' was to be suppressed; the parades to honour Old Major would be abandoned and his skull had already been buried; the flag was to be changed to a plain green. (Remember what it used to include.) The signs are that the future of the animals will be worse than anything they knew under Jones. The final irony comes with the renaming of the farm as Manor Farm.

261 There was the . . .

The final vision presented to Clover's dim, old eyes is of pigs and men melting into an indistinguishable similarity. Does she sense the betrayal that has taken place? Why do you think the author chose such an intensely bitter scene with which to end the book?

262 But they had . . .

The cycle of corruption is complete. What is there to choose between one master and another for the animals? The story ends much as it began with the owners of Animal Farm drinking too much, but this time there is nowhere for the animals to go and hear about an optimistic dream of a new future with a just society. 'Power tends to corrupt, and absolute power corrupts absolutely', but why or how did the animals let it happen? Are there any lessons for us as individuals and for our society to learn from Animal Farm?

Characters
in the novel

This is a very brief overview of each character. You should use it as a starting-point for your own studies of characterization. For each of the aspects of character mentioned you should look in your text for evidence to support or contradict the views expressed here, and indeed, your own views as well.

Know the incidents and conversations which will support and enlarge upon your knowledge of each character. You will find it helpful to select a character and follow the commentary, referring always to the text to read and digest the context of the comment.

Do note the animal characteristics which the author uses and manipulates in his presentation of the inhabitants of Animal Farm; they are part and parcel of the caricature element of the story.

References to characters of the Russian Revolution are for interest only. Remember, you are studying a work of fiction, not the history of the Russian Revolution.

Benjamin

Benjamin is usually represented as a cynic, often one who doubts the good intentions of those around him. Certainly he is a sceptic – one who doubts the truth of any particular theory or fact. Like the other animals, Benjamin learns to read but though he masters the process, he steadfastly refuses to put it to any use. Is he afraid of confirming that his cynicism is justified and thus being forced to act? He is also curiously inactive when he could have helped his only friend, Boxer. Perhaps Orwell is implying that, without some sort of faith or idealism, the intellect is of little real use.

Orwell emphasizes that Benjamin never laughs, when donkeys are known for their braying laugh. Admittedly there is not much to laugh about in Animal Farm, everything is so utterly serious. Perhaps there is a comment here on the joyless nature of so many of our political ideals?

Boxer

Boxer is an enormously strong cart-horse upon whom the work of the farm, and therefore its survival, depends. He is a gentle giant who tries never to hurt anyone. His philosophy is simple and based on the nobility of labour. He is exploited by whoever runs the farm and unwittingly, owing to his crucial importance in the farm work and lack of any sort of perception, plays a part in the exploitation of other animals. It is through his eyes that many of the events are seen.

Boxer represents the idealized worker, not just the Russian peasant, but someone ordinary, decent and totally necessary to the success of any social system. He is the type of person who in a revolution, or extreme political system, is inevitably exploited.

In his lifetime he was used badly, and even in death his maxims 'I must work harder', and 'Napoleon is always right' are flaunted at the other animals.

As Boxer never realized that the ideals of the Rebellion were being corrupted, he is spared the scene of pigs and men becoming indistinguishable to the watching animals.

You should consider what changes occur in Boxer's attitudes during the story. Note, in particular, his change in attitude to injuring those around him, especially as seen in the incidents of the stable-boy he injured, and the dogs who attacked him. One might feel like criticizing Boxer for being so unimaginative in his response to what was happening to his world, but do also realize that there is an implied warning here from the author, on the dulling effects on the spirit of man from a life of ceaseless hard work.

Boxer's part in *Animal Farm* also has something to do with questioning and holding accountable the actions of those in power over us. His life clearly highlights the insensitivity to the workers' needs of those in power and responsible for their welfare.

Clover

Clover is a mother figure in *Animal Farm*. Her good sense, if limited, is sound, and complements Boxer's qualities of simple goodness and strength. More than any other animal she represents sympathy and kindness. She is disturbed in a way that the others are not by some of the terrible events on the farm. For all that, she is a survivor and source of comfort and strength for all. To what extent do the events that occur change her attitudes and perceptions of the realities of the revolution?

The dogs

The dogs represent those secret organizations of police that dispense punishment without being accountable to the mass of the population. There are, and have been, many such organizations in modern history and in many countries. Their purpose is to prop up the authority of those in power and silence any opposition.

Mollie

Mollie, as her rather frivolous name suggests, has a trivial nature and unimportant role in the story. She is phased out in chapter 5. She is as parasitic in her own way as man is on the other animals, which may be why she prefers to ally herself with men. It has been suggested that she represents the aristocracy. Her most useful contribution is as a contrast to Clover. Her life is one of selfish concern with her vanity and safety.

Moses the raven

Moses the raven is a despicable character who, to an extent, represents Orwell's opinion of the organized church, and its historical role in allying itself with the ruler, rather than the people. Orwell's views on organized religion are close to those of Marx, who felt that it undermined the workers' struggle for decent working conditions and justice on earth, by offering a (vain) hope of a better life hereafter. It is a very simplistic view and fails to take any account of the tremendous force for good that religions have exercised and continue to exercise.

Mr Jones

Mr Jones is the immediate reason for the Rebellion in the same way that Czar Nicholas II was, in very simple terms, the cause of the Russian Revolution. He has fallen upon hard times and has some excuse for drunkenness but it becomes necessary for the animals to escape his brutality and neglect. He is the most detailed of the human characters but plays more part in the story in the abstract, than as a believable character.

Muriel the goat

Muriel the goat is one of the cleverer animals who is at Old Major's assembly. She is not one of the long-term survivors. Although she acquires the ability to read, she never learns any sort of discrimination in what she reads. She seems to accept that whatever is written down must be true and does not question at all the alternatives to the Commandments. Be aware of the implied criticism of those who fail to make intelligent use of their capabilities.

What are some of the usual and proverbial qualities one associates with goats?

Napoleon

Napoleon is usually said to represent Stalin the tyrannical ruler of the USSR after the Russian Revolution, but, as his name suggests, this character is made up of the qualities that typify many dictators. 'Napoleonic' has become a synonym for the type of dictatorship which incorporates a personality cult.

A criticism might be that Napoleon has no redeeming features. Orwell could be said to have overstated his case with his study of power and corruption epitomized in Napoleon.

In many ways *Animal Farm* is all about Napoleon's rise to total power. Gradually his character is revealed and is seen to change, wholly for the worse, with his increasing authority over the animals. Lacking the ideas of Old Major and Snowball he is an opportunist and excellent psychologist. His strength of personality more than makes up for his lack of intellect – like so many absolute rulers.

Old Major

Old Major represents both Marx and Lenin in that he introduces the fundamental theories and ideals on which the Rebellion is based. One Marxian theory expressed is that the animals' labour has more intrinsic value than is required for their own needs. The surplus is stolen from him by parasitic man. There is a nice parallel here with the way Napoleon eventually steals the results of the animals' labour for his own needs. Ironically, under man, the farm was less productive and the animals had less stolen from them.

The Lenin trait of Old Major is expressed in the part of Old Major's speech which reduces complex philosophy to fundamental propositions or maxims that all can understand.

There is also a parallel to be drawn between the homage extracted from the animals for his skull and the exhibition of Lenin's embalmed body in Red Square, Moscow.

Pilkington and Frederick

Usually Pilkington is thought to represent the gentleman-farmer type whose farm, Foxwood, which has echoes of craftiness and the landed gentry, is badly managed while he enjoys country sports. Although Pilkington is a very low-key character, there is a strong note of bitterness about the final scene in which he plays quite a dominant part.

Frederick is usually thought to represent a mix of Frederick the Great and Hitler, and his farm Pinchfield to represent Germany. As well as being efficient he is aggressive and extremely cruel to the animals on his farm, whereas Pilkington is just neglectful.

Both have the role of being external threats to the farm, and reminders to the animals of what they have rebelled from and why they are working so hard, rather than being very convincing characterizations.

The sheep

Plainly Orwell has the proverbial sayings about the silliness of sheep in mind when he set out to portray the sheep in the story. They play a crucial role in Napoleon's rise to power. Without the sheep, Napoleon would have had difficulty in rising to such heights of dictatorship. Be aware of how they represent the manipulation of the masses, particularly in situations such as mass meetings where it is difficult for the individual to present opposing views.

Snowball

Snowball is usually said to represent Trotsky in the Russian Revolution. He is a brilliant speaker and was the intellectual inspiration of the Revolution. Snowball genuinely and without thought of himself works for the benefit of all the animals. Orwell parodies some of Snowball's activities, but probably intended Snowball to convey a degree of hope in the story.

Snowball is a crucial character study of the essentially sincere revolutionary who is out-manoeuvred by the ruthless Napoleon. His ideas are misappropriated and his image is tainted and used to oppress the animals he tried to help.

Squealer

Squealer is one of the four pig founders of the new society based upon Animalism. Like Napoleon he is a survivor. We are not quite sure how much of the propaganda he persuaded the working animals to believe is thought out by Napoleon or the other pigs, or by himself. He seems to know when to appear and explain the latest outrage to the animals in an uncanny manner.

Squealer is presented as a fit, quick-moving, little pig, as nimble in mind as in body. He thrives with the growth of the new society and ends high up in the organization and very much at ease in it. Note his physical appearance at the end though. Plainly he enjoys his work, which is essential to the success of Napoleon and the other pigs. Politically he represents the vast public relations, or propaganda, machine of any modern society.

He deals in half-truths and omissions as well as downright lies. He feeds the workers the illusions that help them to endure their harsh existence. His aim is to stop them being conscious of what is happening to them and so to repress any challenge to the pigs.

Mr Whymper

Mr Whymper is one of the human characters who play a minor part in the story. It would seem that he hopes to exploit the situation but ends up doing as Napoleon instructs him to do. Like the other humans he has no particularly redeeming feature and fuels the idea that the Rebellion, however it turned out, was justified in its original conception.

What happens
in each chapter

Chapter 1   Old Major has summoned all the farm animals to a meeting in the big barn, after Mr Jones, the drunken farmer, has gone to bed. At the meeting all the farm animals are told of Old Major's dream, of a Utopian society free from parasitic man. Old Major tells them to prepare for the Rebellion. He emphasizes the need for unity and mutual help and warns them against adopting man's ways when they win their freedom. He teaches them 'Beasts of England' which describes a future ideal society.

Chapter 2   Old Major dies and there is much excited discussion. The pigs convert his ideas into a social system called Animalism which, with some difficulty, the pigs teach to the other farm animals. One day Jones neglects to feed the animals and, quite spontaneously, the animals turn on Jones and his men and drive them from the farm. They destroy all traces of man's oppression of them, decide to turn the farmhouse into a museum, write the Seven Commandments on the barn wall and rename the farm, Animal Farm. While Snowball and the animals get in the harvest, Napoleon takes the cows' milk for himself and the rest of the pigs.

Chapter 3   A bumper harvest is gathered in record time and the summer is a happy one. All the animals work hard, especially Boxer. On Sunday mornings the flag of green, with hoof and horn symbol, is raised and the week's work is planned. Snowball and Napoleon are the leaders and they always disagree with each other. Snowball sets up various committees and organizes literary classes. The sheep learn a new slogan and keep repeating it. Napoleon takes over a litter of puppies and educates them in isolation. The pigs take the apple crop as necessary for 'brainwork'.

Chapter 4   Napoleon and Snowball spread the news of the Rebellion, by pigeons, to neighbouring farm animals. Mr Pilkington of Foxwood and Mr Frederick of Pinchfield, who do not get on with each other, feel threatened by the Rebellion and spread rumours about Animal Farm. Jones and his men try to recapture the farm, but Snowball has anticipated the attack and cleverly ambushes them. Snowball is wounded. A stable-boy is, mistakenly, thought to be killed by Boxer. At the victory celebration the event is called the Battle of the Cowshed and celebrated annually.

Chapter 5   As winter approaches, Mollie, the vain little mare, defects to the side of the humans. In the cold weather the animals plan next season's work with Napoleon and Snowball in constant disagreement. Snowball creates a plan to build a windmill, which could produce power and energy that would do much of the animals' work. He is on the point of winning the animals' vote for the project, when Napoleon signals his bodyguard of the nine grown puppies to chase Snowball off the farm. Napoleon assumes command, abolishes meetings and later claims the idea of the windmill as his own.

Chapter 6   The second year of Animal Farm sees the animals working very hard, including Sundays, and building the windmill. It takes up so much time that the harvest is not so good. Boxer's Herculean labour keeps the windmill project going. As some things cannot be produced by the farm, Napoleon decides to trade with the other farms. This trade is conducted through Mr Whymper, a solicitor. Squealer pacifies the protests of the animals. The pigs move into the farmhouse. In November a storm destroys the half-finished windmill and the absent Snowball is blamed by Napoleon.

Chapter 7   Bitterly cold winter weather prevents work on the windmill and there are food shortages. Whymper is deceived into thinking that the food bins are full and so Animal Farm is in a position to trade. The hens are forced by Napoleon to give up their eggs for sale. There is a witch-hunt for Snowball who is blamed for everything that goes wrong. At one point Boxer challenges the pigs. Later at an assembly Napoleon has a trial of four of the pigs and other animals, who confess to ludicrous crimes and are killed by the dogs, who also unsuccessfully attack Boxer. On the knoll Clover and the other animals try to express their grief in 'Beasts of England' but Squealer tells them it has been replaced by another song.

Chapter 8   The Sixth Commandment is altered to excuse the killings. Napoleon keeps aloof from the animals as a remote leader-figure. Squealer regularly gives out glowing reports of the farm's progress. Napoleon plays off Pilkington and Frederick against each other over the proposed sale of timber. Frederick buys the timber with counterfeit banknotes. He then attacks Animal Farm and blows up the windmill which enrages the animals, who drive off the humans at a great cost of life and injury. Boxer is wounded in what is then known as the Battle of the Windmill. After subdued victory celebrations by the animals, the pigs get drunk on Jones's whisky.

Chapter 9   Boxer begins to age but continues to labour at the building of the windmill. Rations, except for those of the pigs and dogs, are reduced. Thirty-one pigs are born and their privileged education is supervised by Napoleon. Compulsory 'Spontaneous Demonstrations' are held. Squealer reads out figures to show how much better life is now than it was in Jones's day. Moses the raven returns to tell them about Sugarcandy Mountain. Animal Farm becomes a Republic with one candidate for President: Napoleon. Boxer collapses and is taken off to the slaughterhouse. Squealer claims Boxer died in hospital but Benjamin the donkey knows better. There is a grotesque memorial banquet which only the pigs attend.

Chapter 10   Several years have passed; some animals have died but none have retired, although the farm has prospered. No one can remember life before the Rebellion, and they take pride in their unique society. Suddenly the pigs appear walking upright and carrying whips. The sheep have a new slogan and the Seven Commandments are reduced to one. The pigs adopt a human life-style. The final scene shows pigs and men at a party. Napoleon announces that the farm will revert to the original name, Manor Farm. The onlooking animals look from pig to man and back again until they realize that they are exactly alike. The transformation is complete.

Coursework and preparing for the examination

If you wish to gain a certificate in English literature then there is no substitute for studying the text/s on which you are to be examined. If you cannot be bothered to do that, then neither this guide nor any other will be of use to you.

Here we give advice on studying the text, writing a good essay, producing coursework, and sitting the examination. However, if you meet problems you should ask your teacher for help.

Studying the text

No, not just read – study. You must read your text at least twice. Do not dismiss it if you find a first reading difficult or uninteresting. Approach the text with an open mind and you will often find a second reading more enjoyable. When you become a more experienced reader enjoyment usually follows from a close study of the text, when you begin to appreciate both what the author is saying and the skill with which it is said.

Having read the text, you must now study it. We restrict our remarks here to novels and plays, though much of what is said can also be applied to poetry.

1 You will know in full detail all the major incidents in your text, **why**, **where** and **when** they happen, **who** is involved, **what** leads up to them and what follows.

2 You must show that you have an **understanding of the story**, the **characters**, and the **main ideas** which the author is exploring.

3 In a play you must know what happens in each act, and more specifically the organization of the scene structure – how one follows from and builds upon another. Dialogue in both plays and novels is crucial. You must have a detailed knowledge of the major dialogues and soliloquies and the part they play in the development of plot, and the development and drawing of character.

4 When you write about a novel you will not normally be expected to quote or to refer to specific lines but references to incidents and characters must be given, and they must be accurate and specific.

5 In writing about a play you will be expected both to paraphrase dialogue and quote specific lines, always provided, of course, that they are actually contributing something to your essay!

To gain full marks in coursework and/or in an examination you will also be expected to show your own reaction to, and appreciation of, the text studied. The teacher or examiner always welcomes those essays which demonstrate the student's own thoughtful response to the text. Indeed, questions often specify such a requirement, so do participate in those classroom discussions, the debates, class dramatizations of all or selected parts of your text, and the many other activities which enable a class to share and grow in their understanding and feeling for literature.

Making notes
A half-hearted reading of your text, or watching the 'film of the book' will not give you the necessary knowledge to meet the above demands.

As you study the text jot down sequences of events; quotations of note; which events precede and follow the part you are studying; the characters involved; what the part being studied contributes to the plot and your understanding of character and ideas.

Write single words, phrases and short sentences which can be quickly reviewed and which will help you to gain a clear picture of the incident being studied. Make your notes neat and orderly, with headings to indicate chapter, scene, page, incident, character, etc, so that you can quickly find the relevant notes or part of the text when revising.

Writing the essay

Good essays are like good books, in miniature; they are thought about, planned, logically structured, paragraphed, have a clearly defined pattern and development of thought, and are presented clearly – and with neat writing! All of this will be to no avail if the tools you use, i.e. words, and the skill with which you put them together to form your sentences and paragraphs are severely limited.

How good is your general and literary vocabulary? Do you understand and can you make appropriate use of such terms as 'soliloquy', 'character', 'plot', 'mood', 'dramatically effective', 'comedy', 'allusion', 'humour', 'imagery', 'irony', 'paradox', 'anti-climax', 'tragedy'? These are all words which examiners have commented on as being misunderstood by students.

Do you understand 'metaphor', 'simile', 'alliteration'? Can you say what their effect is on you, the reader, and how they enable the author to express himself more effectively than by the use of a different literary device? If you cannot, you are employing your time ineffectively by using them.

You are writing an English literature essay and your writing should be literate and appropriate. Slang, colloquialisms and careless use of words are not tolerated in such essays.

Essays for coursework

The exact number of essays you will have to produce and their length will vary; it depends upon the requirements of the examination board whose course you are following, and whether you will be judged solely on coursework or on a mixture of coursework and examination.

As a guide, however your course is structured, you will be required to provide a folder containing at least ten essays, and from that folder approximately five will be selected for moderation purposes. Of those essays, one will normally have been done in class-time under conditions similar to those of an examination. The essays must cover the complete range of course requirements and be the unaided work of the student. One board specifies that these pieces of continuous writing should be a minimum of 400 words long, and another, a minimum of 500 words long. Ensure that you know what is required for your course, and do not aim for the minimum amount – write a full essay then prune it down if necessary.

Do take care over the presentation of your final folder of coursework. There are many devices on the market which will enable you to bind your work neatly, and in such a way that you can easily insert new pieces. Include a 'Contents' page and a front and back cover to keep your work clean. Ring binders are unsuitable items to hand in for **final** assessment purposes as they are much too bulky.

What sort of coursework essays will you be set? All boards lay down criteria similar to the following for the range of student response to literature that the coursework must cover.

Work must demonstrate that the student:

1 shows an understanding not only of surface meaning but also of a deeper awareness of themes and attitudes;

2 recognizes and appreciates ways in which authors use language;

3 recognizes and appreciates ways in which writers achieve their effects, particularly in how the work is structured and in its characterization;

4 can write imaginatively in exploring and developing ideas so as to communicate a sensitive and informed personal response to what is read.

Much of what is said in the section 'Writing essays in an examination' (below) is relevant here, but for coursework essays you have the advantage of plenty of time to prepare your work – so take advantage of it.

There is no substitute for arguing, discussing and talking about a question on a particular text or theme. Your teacher should give you plenty of opportunity for this in the classroom. Listening to what others say about a subject often opens up for you new ways to look at and respond to it. The same can be said for reading about a topic. Be careful not to copy down slavishly what others say and write. Jot down notes then go away and think about what you have heard, read and written. Make more notes of your own and then start to clarify your own thoughts, feelings and emotions on the subject about which you are writing. Most students make the mistake of doing their coursework essays in a rush – you have time so use it.

Take a great deal of care in planning your work. From all your notes, write a rough draft and then start the task of really perfecting it.

1 Look at your arrangement of paragraphs, is there a logical development of thought or argument? Do the paragraphs need rearranging in order? Does the first or last sentence of any paragraph need redrafting in order to provide a sensible link with the preceding or next paragraph?

2 Look at the pattern of sentences within each paragraph. Are your thoughts and ideas clearly developed and expressed? Have you used any quotations, paraphrases, or references to incidents to support your opinions and ideas? Are those references relevant and apt, or just 'padding'?

3 Look at the words you have used. Try to avoid repeating words in close proximity one to another. Are the words you have used to comment on the text being studied the most appropriate and effective, or just the first ones you thought of?

4 Check your spelling and punctuation.

5 Now write a final draft, the quality of which should reflect the above considerations.

Writing essays in an examination
Read the question. Identify the key words and phrases. Write them down, and as they are dealt with in your essay plan, tick them off.

Plan your essay. Spend about five minutes jotting down ideas; organize your thoughts and ideas into a logical and developing order – a structure is essential to the production of a good essay. Remember, brief, essential notes only!

Write your essay
How long should it be? There is no magic length. What you must do is answer the question set, fully and sensitively in the time allowed. You will probably have about forty minutes to answer an essay question, and within that time you should produce an essay between roughly 350 and 500 words in length. Very short answers will not do justice to the question, very long answers will probably contain much irrelevant information and waste time that should be spent on the next answer.

How much quotation? Use only that which is apt and contributes to the clarity and quality of your answer. No examiner will be impressed by 'padding'.

What will the examiners be looking for in an essay?
1 An answer to the question set, and not a prepared answer to another, albeit slightly similar question done in class.

2 A well-planned, logically structured and paragraphed essay with a beginning, middle and end.

3 Accurate references to plot, character, theme, as required by the question.

4 Appropriate, brief, and if needed, frequent quotation and references to support and demonstrate the comments that you are making in your essay.

5 Evidence that reading the text has prompted in you a personal response to it, as well as some judgment and appreciation of its literary merit.

How do you prepare to do this?

1 During your course you should write between three to five essays on each text.

2 Make good use of class discussion etc, as mentioned in a previous paragraph on page 73.

3 Try to see a live performance of a play. It may help to see a film of a play or book, though be aware that directors sometimes leave out episodes, change their order, or worse, add episodes that are not in the original – so be very careful. In the end, there is no substitute for **reading and studying** the text!

Try the following exercises without referring to any notes or text.

1 Pick a character from your text.

2 Make a list of his/her qualities – both positive and negative ones, or aspects that you cannot quite define. Jot down single words to describe each quality. If you do not know the word you want, use a thesaurus, but use it in conjunction with a dictionary and make sure you are fully aware of the meaning of each word you use.

3 Write a short sentence which identifies one or more places in the text where you think each quality is demonstrated.

4 Jot down any brief quotation, paraphrase of conversation or outline of an incident which shows that quality.

5 Organize the list. Identify groupings which contrast the positive and negative aspects of character.

6 Write a description of that character which makes full use of the material you have just prepared.

7 What do you think of the character you have just described? How has he/she reacted to and coped with the pressures of the other characters, incidents, and the setting of the story? Has he/she changed in any way? In no more than 100 words, including 'evidence' taken from the text, write a balanced assessment of the character, and draw some conclusions.

You should be able to do the above without notes, and without the text, unless you are to take an examination which allows the use of plain texts. In plain text examinations you are allowed to take in a copy of your text. It must be without notes, either your own or the publisher's. The intention is to enable you to consult a text in the examination so as to confirm memory of detail, thus enabling a candidate to quote and refer more accurately in order to illustrate his/her views that more effectively. Examiners will expect a high standard of accurate reference, quotation and comment in a plain text examination.

Sitting the examination

You will have typically between two and five essays to write and you will have roughly 40 minutes, on average, to write each essay.

On each book you have studied, you should have a choice of doing at least one out of two or three essay titles set.

1   **Before sitting the exam**, make sure you are completely clear in your mind that you know exactly how many questions you must answer, which sections of the paper you must tackle, and how many questions you may, or must, attempt on any one book or in any one section of the paper. If you are not sure, ask your teacher.

2   **Always read the instructions** given at the top of your examination paper. They are

there to help you. Take your time, and try to relax – panicking will not help.

3 **Be very clear about timing, and organizing your time.**

(a) Know how long the examination is.
(b) Know how many questions you must do.
(c) Divide (b) into (a) to work out how long you may spend on each question. (Bear in mind that some questions may attract more marks, and should therefore take proportionately more time.)
(d) Keep an eye on the time, and do not spend more than you have allowed for any one question.
(e) If you have spare time at the end you can come back to a question and do more work on it.
(f) Do not be afraid to jot down notes as an aid to memory, but do cross them out carefully after use – a single line will do!

4 **Do not rush the decision** as to which question you are going to answer on a particular text.

(a) Study each question carefully.
(b) Be absolutely sure what each one is asking for.
(c) Make your decision as to which you will answer.

5 **Having decided which question** you will attempt:

(a) jot down the key points of the actual question – use single words or short phrases;
(b) think about how you are going to arrange your answer. Five minutes here, with some notes jotted down will pay dividends later;
(c) write your essay, and keep an eye on the time!

6 **Adopt the same approach** for all questions. Do write answers for the maximum number of questions you are told to attempt. One left out will lose its proportion of the total marks. Remember also, you will never be awarded extra marks, over and above those already allocated, if you write an extra long essay on a particular question.

7 **Do not waste time** on the following:

(a) an extra question – you will get no marks for it;
(b) worrying about how much anyone else is writing, they can't help you!
(c) relaxing at the end with time to spare – you do not have any. Work up to the very moment the invigilator tells you to stop writing. Check and recheck your work, including spelling and punctuation. Every single mark you gain helps, and that last mark might tip the balance between success and failure – the line has to be drawn somewhere.

8 **Help the examiner.**

(a) Do not use red or green pen or pencil on your paper. Examiners usually annotate your script in red and green, and if you use the same colours it will cause unnecessary confusion.
(b) Leave some space between each answer or section of an answer. This could also help you if you remember something you wish to add to your answer when you are checking it.
(c) Number your answers as instructed. If it is question 3 you are doing, do not label it 'C'.
(d) Write neatly. It will help you to communicate effectively with the examiner who is trying to read your script.

Glossary of literary terms

Mere knowledge of the words in this list or other specialist words used when studying literature is not sufficient. You must know when to use a particular term, and be able to describe what it contributes to that part of the work which is being discussed.

For example, merely to label something as being a metaphor does not help an examiner or teacher to assess your response to the work being studied. You must go on to analyse what the literary device contributes to the work. Why did the author use a metaphor at all? Why not some other literary device? What extra sense of feeling or meaning does the metaphor convey to the reader? How effective is it in supporting the author's intention? What was the author's intention, as far as you can judge, in using that metaphor?

Whenever you use a particular literary term you must do so with a purpose and that purpose usually involves an explanation and expansion upon its use. Occasionally you will simply use a literary term 'in passing', as, for example, when you refer to the 'narrator' of a story as opposed to the 'author' – they are not always the same! So please be sure that you understand both the meaning and purpose of each literary term you employ.

This list includes only those words which we feel will assist in helping you to understand the major concepts in play and novel construction. It makes no attempt to be comprehensive. These are the concepts which examiners frequently comment upon as being inadequately grasped by many students. Your teacher will no doubt expand upon this list and introduce you to other literary devices and words within the context of the particular work/s you are studying – the most useful place to experience and explore them and their uses.

Plot This is the plan or story of a play or novel. Just as a body has a skeleton to hold it together, so the plot forms the 'bare bones' of the work of literature in play or novel form. It is however, much more than this. It is arranged in time, so one of the things which encourages us to continue reading is to see what happens next. It deals with causality, that is how one event or incident causes another. It has a sequence, so that in general, we move from the beginning through to the end.

Structure The arrangement and interrelationship of parts in a play or novel are obviously bound up with the plot. An examination of how the author has structured his work will lead us to consider the function of, say, the 43 letters which are such an important part of *Pride and Prejudice*. We would consider the arrangement of the time-sequence in *Wuthering Heights* with its 'flashbacks' and their association with the different narrators of the story. In a play we would look at the scene divisions and how different events are placed in a relationship so as to produce a particular effect; where soliloquies occur so as to inform the audience of a character's innermost emotions and feelings. Do be aware that great works of fiction are not just simply thrown together by their authors. We study a work in detail, admiring its parts and the intricacies of its structure. The reason for a work's greatness has to do with the genius of its author and the care of its construction. Ultimately, though, we do well to remember that it is the work as a whole that we have to judge, not just the parts which make up that whole.

Narrator A narrator tells or relates a story. In *Wuthering Heights* various characters take on the task of narrating the events of the story: Cathy, Heathcliff, etc, as well as being, at other times, central characters taking their part in the story. Sometimes the author will be there, as it were, in person, relating and explaining events. The method adopted in telling the story relates very closely to style and structure.

Style The manner in which something is expressed or performed, considered as separate from its intrinsic content or meaning. It might well be that a lyrical, almost poetical style will be used, for example concentrating on the beauties and contrasts of the natural world as a foil to the narration of the story and creating emotions in the reader which serve to heighten reactions to the events being played out on the page. It might be that the author uses a terse, almost staccato approach to the conveyance of his story. There is no simple route to grasping the variations of style which are to be found between different authors or indeed within one novel. The surest way to appreciate this difference is to read widely and thoughtfully and; to analyse and appreciate the various strategies which an author uses to command our attention.

Character A person represented in a play or story. However, the word also refers to the combination of traits and qualities distinguishing the individual nature of a person or thing. Thus, a characteristic is one such distinguishing quality: in *Pride and Prejudice*, the pride and prejudices of various characters are central to the novel, and these characteristics which are associated with Mr Darcy, Elizabeth, and Lady Catherine in that novel, enable us to begin assessing how a character is reacting to the surrounding events and people. Equally, the lack of a particular trait or characteristic can also tell us much about a character.

Character development In *Pride and Prejudice*, the extent to which Darcy's pride, or Elizabeth's prejudice is altered, the recognition by those characters of such change, and the events of the novel which bring about the changes are central to any exploration of how a character develops, for better or worse.

Irony This is normally taken to be the humorous or mildly sarcastic use of words to imply the opposite of what they say. It also refers to situations and events and thus you will come across references such as prophetic, tragic, and dramatic irony.

Dramatic irony This occurs when the implications of a situation or speech are understood by the audience but not by all or some of the characters in the play or novel. We also class as ironic words spoken innocently but which a later event proves either to have been mistaken or to have prophesied that event. When we read in the play *Macbeth*:

> *Macbeth*
> Tonight we hold a solemn supper, sir,
> And I'll request your presence.
>
> *Banquo*
> Let your highness
> Command upon me, to the which my duties
> Are with a most indissoluble tie
> Forever knit.

we, as the audience, will shortly have revealed to us the irony of Macbeth's words. He does not expect Banquo to attend the supper as he plans to have Banquo murdered before the supper occurs. However, what Macbeth does not know is the prophetic irony of Banquo's response. His 'duties. . . a most indissoluble tie' will be fulfilled by his appearance at the supper as a ghost – something Macbeth certainly did not forsee or welcome, and which Banquo most certainly did not have in mind!

Tragedy This is usually applied to a play in which the main character, usually a person of importance and outstanding personal qualities, falls to disaster through the combination of personal failing and circumstances with which he cannot deal. Such tragic happenings may also be central to a novel. In *The Mayor of Casterbridge*, flaws in Henchard's character are partly responsible for his downfall and eventual death.

In Shakespeare's plays, *Macbeth* and *Othello*, the tragic heroes from which the two plays take their names, are both highly respected and honoured men who have proven their outstanding personal qualities. Macbeth, driven on by his ambition and that of his very determined wife, kills his king. It leads to civil war in his country, to his own eventual downfall and death, and to his wife's suicide. Othello, driven to an insane jealousy by the cunning of his lieutenant, Iago, murders his own innocent wife and commits suicide.

Satire   Where topical issues, folly or evil are held up to scorn by means of ridicule and irony – the satire may be subtle or openly abusive.

In *Animal Farm*, George Orwell used the rebellion of the animals against their oppressive owner to satirize the excesses of the Russian revolution at the beginning of the 20th century. It would be a mistake, however, to see the satire as applicable only to that event. There is a much wider application of that satire to political and social happenings both before and since the Russian revolution and in all parts of the world.

Images   An image is a mental representation or picture. One that constantly recurs in *Macbeth* is clothing, sometimes through double meanings of words: 'he seems rapt withal', 'Why do you dress me in borrowed robes?', 'look how our partner's rapt', 'Like our strange garments, cleave not to their mould', 'Whiles I stood rapt in the wonder of it', 'which would be worn now in their newest gloss', 'Was the hope drunk Wherein you dressed yourself?', 'Lest our old robes sit easier than our new.', 'like a giant's robe upon a dwarfish thief'. All these images serve to highlight and comment upon aspects of Macbeth's behaviour and character. In Act 5, Macbeth the loyal soldier who was so honoured by his king at the start of the play, struggles to regain some small shred of his self-respect. Three times he calls to Seyton for his armour, and finally moves toward his destiny with the words 'Blow wind, come wrack, At least we'll die with harness on our back' – his own armour, not the borrowed robes of a king he murdered.

Do remember that knowing a list of images is not sufficient. You must be able to interpret them and comment upon the contribution they make to the story being told.

Theme   A unifying idea, image or motif, repeated or developed throughout a work.

In *Pride and Prejudice*, a major theme is marriage. During the course of the novel we are shown various views of and attitudes towards marriage. We actually witness the relationships of four different couples through their courtship, engagement and eventual marriage. Through those events and the examples presented to us in the novel of other already married couples, the author engages in a thorough exploration of the theme.

This list is necessarily short. There are whole books devoted to the explanation of literary terms. Some concepts, like style, need to be experienced and discussed in a group setting with plenty of examples in front of you. Others, such as dramatic irony, need keen observation from the student and a close knowledge of the text to appreciate their significance and existence. All such specialist terms are well worth knowing. But they should be used only if they enable you to more effectively express your knowledge and appreciation of the work being studied.

Titles in the series

GCSE

Pride and Prejudice

To Kill A Mockingbird

Romeo and Juliet

The Mayor of Casterbridge

Macbeth

Far from the Madding Crowd

A Midsummer Night's Dream

Pygmalion

Wuthering Heights

Animal Farm

Lord of the Flies

Great Expectations

Of Mice and Men

A Man for All Seasons

Jane Eyre

The Crucible

Hobson's Choice

An Inspector Calls

A Level

Coriolanus

The Pardoner's Tale